IN ONE LIFETIME

With Best Wishes To You Both

Theresa

By: Theresa Shanoha

Note for Librarians: A cataloguing record for this book is available from Library and Archives
Canada at www.collectionscanada.ca/amicus/index-e.html
ISBN 1-4120-9629-4

Printed in Victoria, BC, Canada. Printed on paper with minimum 30% recycled fibre.
Trafford's print shop runs on "green energy" from solar, wind and other environmentally-friendly power sources.

PUBLISHING™

Offices in Canada, USA, Ireland and UK

Book sales for North America and international:
Trafford Publishing, 6E–2333 Government St.,
Victoria, BC V8T 4P4 CANADA
phone 250 383 6864 (toll-free 1 888 232 4444)
fax 250 383 6804; email to orders@trafford.com
Book sales in Europe:
Trafford Publishing (UK) Limited, 9 Park End Street, 2nd Floor
Oxford, UK OX1 1HH UNITED KINGDOM
phone +44 (0)1865 722 113 (local rate 0845 230 9601)
facsimile +44 (0)1865 722 868; info.uk@trafford.com
Order online at:
trafford.com/06-1385
10 9 8 7 6 5 4 3 2

DEDICATED TO:

To All Abused Spouses in the past and in
the future. May GOD watch over
everyone.

INTRODUCTION

This is a story of my life from birth to present day. This just has to be told, reason, I have been through two very abusive marriages. One was easily recognizable because it was both physical and verbal. This left me distorted mentally for a very long period of time. Also, in general, feeling hopeless and inadequate, I needed and should have received some guidance but in those early days, there was little or no help whatever.

The second marriage became verbally abusive after my Husband's epilepsy showed its face. It was very subtle at first and after a while, had learned to live with it as if it were normal, of course it was not. This is the worst kind of abuse; it literally sneaks up on you. The whole thing started when my youngest Son was only four and a half years of age. He was not only my Son but became my very best friend. It is at a long distance now, as I live in Winnipeg and he and his lovely family lives in Sudbury, Ontario. Now do not get me wrong, there were many wonderful times in my life as well as the abuse.

Only hope this story will help those whom I wish it to, namely, anyone who is in the same or similar situation. Though the book will be sad at times, it will also be very enjoyable and happy. May this book be a good read for those who decide to purchase it?

Now this is so very important to me, and also to everyone who has found themselves in this situation. God Bless All Of You! May you find your way back to normalcy and be mentally prepared for the life ahead of you.

Help will be needed by you, this I truly do know. You are probably not aware of just how much you have been suffering, all you know is, that this cannot continue any longer. Your personality is literally dying inside of you. Please get the much needed help; whether you think you need it or not. Obtain help from a Social Worker, Psychiatrist, Priest and Preacher or even from your family Physician. He or she will guide you to the right person to take care of all your problems. There is no shame in receiving this kind of assistance, so please believe me; it is worth the peace of mind and heart.

At first you may think you can go it alone, just take my word for it, you cannot; you will probably end up with a nervous breakdown if you try. You are likely too stressed out to really realize what is happening; only others that are listening to you will recognize your mental and physical anguish. Even if you do recognize the situation you are in, you still need to seek the help; no one has ever been able to go it alone without a problem.

THE AUTHOR!
Theresa Shanoha

INDEX

Chapter	Page
One – From Birth	1
Two - Our Grandfather.	9
Three - Up to my first marriage.	13
Four - My first abusive Marriage.	17
Five - Sons illness and divorce.	34
Six – My Second Marriage and Adoptions	43
Seven –My Mother came to Winnipeg.	67
Eight - Husband into Professional Soccer	74
Nine - Ted's marriage and divorce	90
Ten - My heart attack.	96
Eleven - My Husbands heart attack.	106
Twelve -Youngest Sons Wedding.	113
Thirteen - Jim's down grading of health.	121
Fourteen - The Birth of our Two Grandsons.	132
Fifteen – Change of Doctors to now.	145

Chapter One

The beginning of my life started in the early hours of December 14th. 1933. My parents lived in a log cabin just outside of St. Johns County, St. Johns, New Brunswick, Canada. This is where I was born. There was no one to help my Mother during my delivery, not even her Doctor; he came way too late, well after my birth. My Mother told me this when I grew up, and that my birth was her fifth full term pregnancy. The other four pregnancies were all still born, three girls and one boy.

I was far too young to remember ever living in the log cabin. At one and a half years of age, I had contracted tuberculoses in my lower abdomen; my tummy was absolutely huge according to my Mother. Apparently at that time I was severely undernourished which probably contributed to the other problem. They had to put me into hospital for over a year. There were needles put into my abdomen, and they were attached to a pump to remove the fluid that had built up in there. That is how they took care of it in those days. Once a month they would remove the old needles and put in new ones, in a different area of course. This was so that no infection would occur.

My Mother also told me at one time, during the stay in the hospital, that I would climb up the back of the crib and look out the hallway windows. When I was satisfied at what was there, I would then jump down squealing with delight, in other words a real brat. My diet was outrageous though; there was raw fish with chocolate syrup over it, and then raw eggs with the same chocolate syrup over them. No wonder I would not eat any kind of fish or eggs for many years. It was not until I was all grown up, and did my own cooking, that I dared to try and eat them again. Fish and eggs are not really bad as long as they are fully cooked.

During my stay in hospital, my Mother gave birth to a second child carried full term. It was a little girl, she was healthy, her name is Martina and she was born on June 23rd. 1935. My sister Martina was the last born to our Parents.

When I was only four and a half years of age, our parents' marriage had broken up; there was a lot of hatred and bitterness. Our beloved Mother was always suspicious of our Father, maybe with good reason, who knows? We were never told what had happened. It was a good thing that it did not last any longer, as suspicion and jealousies have no place in a marriage. It would only continue to tear the both of them apart.

Our Mother decided to pack us up and move us to Vancouver, British Columbia; this is where our Grandparents were living. We traveled by bus, went across the U. S. Border, along the northern part of the United States to Seattle Washington. Once there we again crossed the border to go to Vancouver, B.C.

Upon our arrival in Vancouver, we stayed in a Hotel and ate our meals at the then White Restaurant, nothing like today's restaurant. When the money ran out, our Mother applied and received Welfare assistance. In those days, Welfare had their own clothing and shoe stores as well as old homes for their recipients. We were assigned a house on Hastings Street in North Burnaby; that was on the outskirts of Vancouver. Our place had three rooms, a small kitchen with a sink and cold running water, a table with three mismatched chairs, also a wood and coal stove. The bed sitting room had a davenport for our Mother to sleep on, a dresser and last of all, a bedroom with a double bed along with a mattress where Martina and I slept.

The washroom was an outhouse with plenty of rats, what we needed was a cat to protect us from the rats. It was not long before Martina and I found a cat, it was only a kitten and it was being mistreated by some children. They had it by the tail and were hitting the side of the house with it; that was utterly cruel. Thank goodness the little one was only stunned for awhile. Martina and I decided we would take the kitten home, of course our Mother said no but we kept it anyway, that is kids for you.

Our cat saved our Mother from being attacked by a rat; it was on her chest while she was sleeping. Outside the window, our cat made such a ruckus that it woke our Mother up; that cat did that many times. Rats have no fear of humans and would not hesitate chewing on you.

Martina and I decided to name our cat "Tiger" because he had stripes, not original but logical. He was so grateful to us that, he would catch rats at night and pile them up at the back door for a present. Our Mother was surprised at how good the cat was, that she in turn treated him with love and affection.

When our Mother wanted to do the dishes, wash clothes or give us a bath; she would fill a large copper boiler with water and bring it to a boil on the stove. Once a week she would do the wash, boil the whites in the boiler along with shredded bars of Sunlight soap. Later she would scrub them with a brush on a scrubbing board. She used the same metal tub that we had our baths in. Our Mother did a great job on the clothes; we were equally as clean as all the other children whose parents had wringer washing machines.

On our bath days, which were usually on a Sunday evening, she would again heat the water up the same way. Our Mother would then pour it into the metal tub; then add cold water so we could get into the tub without scalding ourselves. We all used the same water, we were always clean no matter what; it was a rough time as well as a good time. The only problem was, the harder our Mother had to work, the more bitter she became. In Mother's bitterness she found it very difficult to demonstrate her love for us. We knew it was there though and loved her anyway.

When it was time for me to start going to school, Mother received my basic clothing and shoes from the Welfare shops. The next year, when Martina started school, Mother did the same thing. There was one difference though, she went looking for work and found a job doing housework for an Official of the City. At the same time, the Welfare Department let her pay a token rent until she was able to find another place to move to. It was quite awhile before Mother was able to save enough money to pay for another place; wages were very meagre at the time.

One day her boss's wife asked our Mother to do the laundry; she complied and went downstairs to the basement where the laundry room was. She first sorted all the laundry and put some of the clothes into a wringer washer. While doing this, Mother did not notice the water on the floor nor did she notice that the wire was lying in it. This wire had a bare spot on it which would give no protection against the electrical current. She added the soap and water to the machine; she started it up, but remembers nothing from that moment.

Our Mother later woke up in the hospital as she had received a whopping shock. Her hair had turned completely white and all of her teeth were loose. The teeth had to be removed as they were very painful and she later received dentures to replace them. To top this, she was fired from her job because of negligence and had a hospital bill to pay. In those days, you had to pay for all your hospital stays, all her savings went to pay that bill. Blue collar workers had little or no rights during that period of time, you had to do the best that you could and it just was not easy. Even at that, nothing deterred her, she went out and got more housekeeping jobs at first. Later she found work in a sewing factory, in those days it was a real sweat shop, still it was better than no job at all.

All during this time our Mother planted a garden so that we would have plenty of fresh vegetables. For the fresh fruit in our lives it all came from our Grandparents orchard, they had apples, pears, cherries and grapes. What we could not eat fresh Mother would can and thus we had plenty during the winter months. She had true grit maybe that is where I received mine from, thank goodness that the bitterness is not a part of me, though sometimes I do wonder.

It was during this time that our Mother used to make all of our clothes. Not in the way that you may think, but she would go to the special stores and purchase old used uniforms and greatcoats of the Army, Navy and the Air Force. This cost her very little money; she would bring the items home and take them apart. Once that was done she would then wash them out by hand as they were pure wool. When dry, she would steam press them, pin patterns to them on the right side and they ended up as a dress or a coat for Martina and me. The underside was now the right side because the fabric was sun bleached. She would put different coloured trims on them, and we were dressed like no one else ever was, beautiful. It was then that I swore that I would never become a dressmaker because of all the hard work she would put into her sewing.

Well you guessed it, that is exactly what I had become, a good seamstress, actually a perfectionist at it. Nothing I made ever left me needing to be changed or repaired. It was then that I became aware of the wonderful feeling I received in creating something from nothing. The adrenalin rush is very high, there is nothing like it and it is all natural, not drug or alcohol induced. When one is finished making it and putting on any additional trims, it was absolutely perfect and beautiful. I then understood what our Mother felt when she made us clothing.

It was shortly after that, that Mother asked our Grandparents if she could rent to own the house they owned on Albert Street, the place was only block away from where we were living. They said okay and we made the move by wagon, the same wagon our Grandfather used to collect wood for his home. We moved all our meagre possessions in no time at all to what we saw as a mansion. This was in the eyes of children; of course it was not that at all.

There was a wood and coal stove already there, hooked up to it was a water tank that became hot when the stove was in use; that meant hot running water, marvellous. We had a full bathroom inside our home, no rats anywhere. Tiger our cat took to hunting down mice instead; there were plenty of them around. He made quick work of them; that was an easy job for our cat. The kitchen was small but a perfect size for us; we had a dining-living room and two full bedrooms as well as a full basement. The basement had no concrete floor, it was all earth.

Chapter Two

As we got older, our Grandfather taught us how to chop and saw wood. He would not take any nonsense either; he threatened me with the razor strop a few times as I loved to play around. After the last threat, I thought better of it and buckled down to business. Because I had learned so well, it became my permanent job to get up in the morning; start the fire in the stove, warm up the house and then we would have our breakfast. Our Mother would go to work and we would go to school.

I must tell you about our Grandfather, he was closer to me than my own Father because he was always there for me. He would take me on wood collecting jaunts; we had a lot of fun together. I would collect the sap from the trees and chew it like gum; we could not afford the luxury of gum; sap was good enough for us. Sap had a woody taste, sometimes even a little bitter; it all depended on what tree it came from. We would pretend that it tasted like mint or cherries; what an imagination a child has. Oh yes, by the way, sap and the bark of trees make good toothbrushes and cleaner, it was also less expensive than baking soda or toothpaste, don't you agree? It was on these trips that Grandfather taught us more about wildlife than any book ever did; he was ever so special to us.

We also learned that Grandfather never trusted radios or music machines of any kind, never were told why though, I guess it was just his thing. He only liked live music like a choir, religious music was all his favourites and it is mine too. It was when we found an old record player in his barn that played music tubes; we found the music was truly enjoyable. There were tubes that had "Bye-Bye Blackbird," "The Lord's Prayer," "You are My Sunshine," as well as many waltzes and lullabys. You had to wind it up to play a full tube of music on the player; old fashioned but a lot of fun. Of course the music had a lot of static and scratchy noises, as a child it was still very enjoyable.

It was on one of those days that we were listening to the music that our Grandfather overheard us; he was really very angry and smashed both the record player and all the tubes right in front of us. We were terribly upset by this but even at that we still loved him dearly; he was far more important to us than the record player or tubes. He was oh so special to me.

One day, when I was at his home; he had disposed of a chicken by chopping off its head. Much to my horror, it ran around in circles until it expired. Our Grandfather explained to me that, this was a necessary thing and that we needed food to live on, this was one of the many ways to get it. It did bother me for awhile. Our Mother and Grandmother enlisted my help in cleaning the insides of the bird and plucking out all the pin feathers. Even today I am squeamish about doing this job; that is why I now get all my birds "dressed" as they call it.

On another day, over at Grandfather's home; I had come across a garter snake, I screamed and took off. He told me that the snake was just as afraid of me and it had slithered off in the opposite direction. As a girl, I never did get over being afraid of snakes. It did not help the phobia to disappear when little boys loved to swing them at me. Yes I know garter snakes are not poisonous but there are just some things that we do not ever get used to.

Another time Grandfather asked me to change a fuse in his basement as he was not able to do so at that time. I asked him if the power was turned off and he assured me that it was. To reach the fuse box, I stood on a stool to take out the old fuse. That was when I received a shock which made me very angry. Needless to say that I used every swear word that was in my vocabulary; that really shocked my Grandparents. As it turned out, the last time that he changed the fuse, he had put a penny underneath it to make it last longer. It did that alright, even though it was shut off it still held a charge and that was what hit me. I never used bad language on our Grandparents again; I did apologize for doing so and it was accepted. It was during this time that Grandfather had lost one of his legs to Gangrene; that is why he could not change that fuse. He was a Diabetic; I learned a lot about diabetes from them. Eventually, he was measured for and fitted with a leg prosthesis so that he could walk again. It had taken a lot of begging on the familys' part to get him to accept such a thing.

It was after we moved into the house on Albert Street that our Grandfather came over to cut down the login berry vines that were growing up the front of the house. Our Grandfather climbed the ladder while I held it in place so it would not slide. What concerned me was his good leg and I asked him to be careful, please do not slip on a ladder rung, he promised to be very careful. He trimmed off most of the vines when he did slip on one of the rungs, it did hurt him; it was already too late. That slip had cut the circulation to his foot and gangrene had set in; he later lost that leg. From then on, our Grandfather was no more; by that I mean, he had shut his mind down and never spoke again. That was truly heart breaking. That is one day forever in my memory. When I find anyone who has diabetes, I have to warn them about their feet. You would be surprised at how many diabetics do not listen or pay any attention to their feet.

Chapter Three

--13--

Eventually our Mother had a cleaned out oil drum converted into a furnace, it worked really great. You could put kindling in to start the fire and then add the coal slowly so as not to smother the embers. The fire would burn all day making the house nice and cozy. It was like that all during the cold days. I would only have load the furnace in the mornings and again at night; it put out great heat. For a long time my job was to take care of both the stove and furnace every day.

One day our Mother decided to go to an Estate Sale that someone had told her about. She came home with a truck load of furniture that had cost her only $100.00. Of course I can say that now but, in those days it was a lot of money for someone to have saved. There was a kitchen set, four chairs and a table. A dining room set with six chairs and an oblong table with a buffet. A living room set; a couch with a chair to match. There was a bedroom suite with a double bed and mattress, a double dresser with a mirror, also one other regular sized dresser and a night stand. To top this off, she received a vacuum cleaner and a wringer washer. This all made us feel excited and rich; far from the truth.

It was at this time that it was decided that I could no longer do any of the housework or the washing. Apparently I was not capable of running the machines.

It was okay when I went down on my knees to scrub the floor with a scrubbing brush and use a scrubbing board to do the laundry. At that time it made me super angry but have long since recovered from it, all kids do. Roll reversal is often a painful experience. Now it is in the past and the past is what my book is all about.

Both my sister Martina and I went to High School but only until we completed grade 10. That summer I was sixteen and a half years old, I had decided that going to work was the best thing. I just hated school and saw no future in continuing; have long since regretted that decision. My first job was with an automotive sales business. From my earnings I paid for room and board. Later I purchase a watch for Mother, she liked that very much.

The following year, my sister Martina quit school and joined the armed forces. She met her one and only Husband and soul mate there, they are still happily married. They produced two boys and a girl, her name is also Martina and she is an extremely talented artist. This niece of mine makes a good living at what she does. My sister's Sons, Raymond and Steven presented her with three Grandchildren, my Sister is very proud of. I do not blame her as they really are great children. The terrible part of all this is, if I passed any one of them on the street, not only would I not know them, they would not know me. Just have to go for a visit one of these days and reacquaint myself with everyone. Will have to call Marty on the phone one day and make arrangements, I love her dearly.

To get on with my story, when I was eighteen years old, I met a handsome young man named Robert and fell in love with him. He was poor, that did not matter to me because at that time, I thought love could overcome all barriers and problems, well it does not. I was only fooling myself and did not know it, teenagers who think they know everything, I was one of them. We did have some wonderful times together while he was courting me.

One of those times, I had received the opportunity to go on a large tug boat ride. You know the kind, the big ones that guide ocean liners and tankers into our harbours. We went from Burrard Inlet in Vancouver to Nanoose Bay on Vancouver Island. While on this tug boat I found it was extremely damp and the walls were always wet. It probably was because the boat was all metal, it draws the moisture off the water, I'm no scientist but it just seems logical. Most of the time on that ride, I was shivering, it just was not possible for me to get warm at all.

On our return, the Skipper of the tug allowed me to steer the boat. Upon our arrival in Burrard Inlet the radio blasted out that we could not dock at the usual pier. Apparently a drunk driver drove off the end of the pier, he was lucky because he only ended up with wet clothes and chills.

The problem was that we had to stay out in the inlet until morning before they had cleared the area for us to dock. The other problem for me was, there was no phone at home so I could not get in touch and let Mother know where I was. She did not like telephones and thought they were a useless expense. She also thought they were too expensive and found that she could not afford to have one. I must tell you that because of not letting her know where I was, made her extremely angry, as a matter of fact she was downright furious. Mother accused me of a lot of not so nice things, and of course being a smart mouth, I said: "Yah sure, whatever you say, I'm no longer a virgin." Of course that just was not true, as a teenager I was just plain foolish, it was only to hurt Mother's feelings.

This caused a very large rift between us. I later regretted what I had said with all of my heart. I don't recommend such foolishness by anyone, it is so very painful. Shortly after that incident, I rented a small furnished apartment and moved away from our Mothers'. That was a very lonely move; I do not recommend that under any circumstances, it should always be planned out carefully and with a good feeling with ones' parents. This situation only made me jump into a marriage before I was ready. If I had thought about it a little longer and not let my heart rule my head, I probably would not have been married. I probably would not be writing this book either, who knows?

Chapter Four

For our Wedding, my Aunt Evelyn loaned me a very nice teal suit, a white blouse with a ruffle in front, a little black pillbox hat. A pair of black gloves and black high heeled shoes, as you can see, my Aunt was my size all around. Actually that was fortunate otherwise I would not have had a nice outfit to get married in. Bob and I tied the knot in a Chapel at an Anglican Church with my Aunt and her family in attendance. We did have pictures taken by a professional photographer but never did buy them. We could not afford them and I have no idea what they looked like either.

At first it was a very loving relationship, a lot of play wrestling around and just general mischief on each other like spraying water from spray bottles. It really was a playful time, much like two children, wished it could have lasted and life would have been much pleasanter. Just remembering everything at that time makes me smile so it was not a total lost cause, some happiness was there.

One day Bob asked me to go with him on a small tug that he was working on; I was game and went along. He was towing a large quantity of logs tethered together with chains. As we were getting close to the Second Narrows Bridge, a large ship was sailing by causing a very large swell. I was steering the tug and the swell made it very difficult for me to do. Bob was at the tow line with a large and very sharp axe ready to cut the tow line if it became necessary. Well for some reason, he froze and would not listen to me. I ended up having to turn the wheel hard over so as not to be dragged down by the undertow of the swell. When we finally did get back to the dock with the tow intact; Bob quit his job as he was scared to death over what had happened. Bob never did work on any kind of boat again; that was truly a shame as he had his ticket to run a small tug. He could have written his Captains papers, all he had to do is keep control of his head and not panic. If he had of followed through, his life would have been much easier. There were times that some of the good qualities of his personality showed through.

That was also the first time he showed his true colours so to speak and took it out on me. We were always short of money and what I was earning was just not enough for us to get by on. There was always something he wanted but we really could not afford to buy. He found another job in a warehouse for a while and we found it a little easier going. This was not to his satisfaction though as he wanted more fun; you know, parties and such.

It was on one of these Saturdays that he told me about a friend of his who was having a house party. Bob wanted to go to it so I agreed, I was game to try and have a little fun as long as it was not going to cost us a lot. It really does no hurt to take time and enjoy life a little bit.

This friend's home was in North Vancouver and it was one of those old houses like the one I now live in. The difference being, that house was a two story home with a full basement. My home that I now live in is a bungalow with a part basement and over 100 years old. When we arrived there and walked in the front door, I was immediately hit with a fear; it literally took my breath away. I told Bob that I had to leave but he forced me to stay awhile.

As time carried on, I continued to get sicker; Bob had no choice but to take me home. This was not before I told him and his friends that though I had never been in that house before, I knew what the upstairs looked like. I described the wallpaper in the two bedrooms and the colours in the bathroom. It was a surprise to his friend because those rooms were exactly what I had described. They had just finished stripping the wall paper and painted everything, how could I possibly know that. Of course I still do not know how, the rooms were just in my head. All I know is that there was this feeling of dread; this premonition was making me feel very ill and I just had to leave.

Once I left the house, I could breathe properly again and my stomach settled down, the fear did not leave me. The next morning, we heard the news that the house had burned down along with Bob's friends. A premonition is a real scary thing when it hits you, especially when you have never had one before.

After that I was very leery about going to a house party, when we did, nine times out of ten, I would leave and Bob would end up staying. As for throwing a party at our place, I only did that once as the mess from others being drunk was something that was not very nice. I did not like it when they drank too much and were ill along with the arguments that ensued. By refusing to have such house parties I only managed to make Bob angry. He would end up lashing out at me again and I would receive another black eye. There many bruises throughout my body and it just made me look like someone's punching bag. Still and all, I would not put out the money for such foolishness when the bills had to be paid. Besides that we still had to eat, beer and crackers does not make for a good diet, agreed?

Smart little me thought that just maybe having a baby would make a difference and salvage our marriage. Boy was I ever wrong, it really only continued to drive us farther and farther apart. I know that I am not the only one who has made that mistake and I will probably not be the last, I can only hope someone will learn from my mistakes.

It was during this time period that Bob decided to join one of the Armed Forces Reserves and that would keep him busy at least two nights a week. Reason being, he took on the task of being a teacher to the cadets, he knew how to play the drums and wished to teach them to do the same. Often he would bring home these cadets with their drumsticks and I would have them trying to play the drums on my wooden furniture. At first it almost drove me crazy. After a while, I watched and learned how to play the drums too, with me it was super easy. With the cadets it was super hard; a lot of them had no rhythm in their beings.

Once I got into it, I helped out with the teaching of the drums, I really did enjoy doing so, there must have been a bit of the music in me. Most of those cadets were so good at it, that they were allowed to play the drums at dress parades and Remembrance Day parades. It was at these times that I felt proud of them and this was my reward for my efforts. After classes I would make them hot chocolate and always made sure that it was in my cupboards just for them. My only hope is these same young men turned out to be really good adults and had happy lives.

When I became pregnant it was at one of the hardest times of my life. Bob was out of work and at that particular time a job was hard to find. We were very short of money and living on Salvation Army food vouchers; it was because of this that I never really enjoyed my pregnancy like most Mothers do. Being on the receiving end of the verbal abuse at that time did not make it any easier either. There were many times that all we had in the apartment were; onions, peanut butter and bread, it was better than nothing. Thank

God for the Salvation Army, they came to our rescue many times when we needed them.   .

At that time, when it was most difficult to find something to eat, Bob brought home a young lady named Lorraine and her young eighteen month old Son. This little boy was severely undernourished; all he had been living on was bread and butter. Lorraine was destitute and needed someone to take care of her child for a few weeks until she found a job and a place to go. Well I took care of the little fellow the best I could; it was very difficult. As you know food was a scarce commodity in our place, it was only the barest of necessities.

When Bob went to the grocers, he would talk him into allowing him to get tobacco and cigarette papers. This would make it even harder to get enough milk, bread and other general needs to survive. I must tell you that I was also a smoker at that time but I was different in one sense. To me eating was much more important, just a case of will power. Sometimes the grocer would give me day old goods and charge less for it; that extended the use of the vouchers. At least this way, we were able to have a little more to eat and in some cases, it was even more nourishing.

At one time, the Salvation Army offered me a job which I had to refuse. When I told them why, they were very surprised and apologized for being so ignorant. That was okay by me as no one had informed

them that I was very pregnant. You see, it was a
cleaning job, if it had of been an office job, it would
have been no problem at all; I would have gladly taken
the work. It was just too far into my pregnancy to take
such a chance. Since then, I have been grateful to the
Salvation Army for coming to my rescue not only once
but twice. Since then I have donated clothing and
money to them whenever it was financially feasible.

About three weeks later, on June 9th. 1954, I
ended up in hospital. It was after midnight when they
took me into the labour room. The attending Nurse
said to me: "Don't you wish you could shit bricks?" I
answered her: "It would certainly be a lot easier than
this, don't you think?" In those days husbands were not
allowed into the labour or delivery rooms. If they had
of been, I very likely would have hated Bob at that
moment in time, even though it was my fault for
wanting a baby. Who says one has to be logical about
this?   I have often wondered how many wives have
become defensive at this time in their lives, many I bet.

In the delivery room, my Doctor told me that it
was a breach birth and that the baby needed to be
turned. Even at that, because my pelvic area was so
small, the Doctor would have to make an incision. He
asked me what side I would like to have it done on; I
told him that it did not make a difference to me, just get
it over with. The Doctor turned my baby, knocked me
out with ether at that time and delivered my son; he was

six pounds, seven ounces. The baby was also twenty-seven inches long; we named him Theodore Robert, to me he was the most beautiful baby in the world. As you know, all Mothers think their child is the most beautiful.

At that time, the Salvation Army came to our rescue a second time; they gave us extra food vouchers for baby goods and wool with knitting needles so that I could make our son some warm outfits. When we took our son home, we still had Lorraine's little boy to care for; I had a real job on my hands. While I was in hospital, my Mother had taken care of the little fellow for me, she did an excellent job; thank GOD for Mothers.

It was about two weeks later that I found myself a job with a truck building firm; had to start in another two weeks. Upon returning to our apartment, I phoned an organization who places children with good families for adoption or foster care; this was for Lorraine's little boy. There were many questions, one most prominent in my mind was: "Has the Mother been in touch with you in any way at all?" I had to answer no as I never did hear from Lorraine again. I emphasized the fact that the little boy needed a home with lots of love. The boy was also in dire need of new clothes. Reason being, he had very little to wear, not even a coat or parka. My idea was that just maybe, a farm family might be the best placement for him. This little fellow was always in a very small room for most of his young life. A farm would have good fresh food, lots of space to play; animals to get to know, in general, a very good life for a little boy.

About ten days after this, the organization called me back, they had found a family that lived on a farm. They asked if they could come and pick the boy up; of course they could. When they arrived, they had brought all his new clothes with them so that I could see that he would be okay. In another month, the organization contacted me once again, this time it was to let me know how the little fellow was doing. Apparently he was doing real well; that he loved his new home. Above all, not only was he well fed but being loved like never before. The family wanted to adopt him; what better news could I get about him, none. Lorraine never did contact us or try to get in touch with the organization to find out how her child was doing, what a shame! Either she did not care at all, which is possible but doubtful, or something must have happened to her where she could not get in touch with anyone. This I cannot imagine what though. I have often wondered what that little guy had become.

It was shortly after that I found us a house in Vancouver with reasonable rent and it was also close to my new job. Because there were no nursery schools at that time; I had no choice but to hire a live-in babysitter. It was that or search for someone who was willing to take care of my son in their own home. Hiring a live-in was the best idea. Our child would not have to be taken to another residence; he would always be where he belonged.

During this period of time, my so called husband was running around with other foolish pretty girls. He always said he was looking for a job and never even had an interview, how does one find work cuddled up in bed with someone else? I went to see my Boss and asked him if there was a chance that he could find Bob work. I was having difficulty getting along on the money I was earning and that having another little mouth to feed never made it any easier. My Boss found work for him, a job he could not refuse. Bob needed money also as he was not able to get any from me, there just was none to spare.

He was real angry that I did this; he told me that I was treating him like an incompetent person. Well he was right about feeling that way, as not only did I think he was an incompetent person but a very lazy one too. To me my first priority was our son, he needed care and good food so whether Bob liked it or not, he had a job. Truly believe that if there was anyone else in the same situation and if they could get their Boss to help out, I am sure they would do so.

Anyway it was a job that Bob had to drive an eighteen wheeler; he had to be trained to do this. For a while, it was a minimum wage job until he accomplished what was required of him. Bob loved the job at first; it gave him a lot of freedom to drive to places that he had never been before and still get paid for it. He did give me a lot of bad mouth for a while because of his deflated ego, believe it or not, I did understand. He would not hit me while he had that job at first as he did not want to lose it. My Boss would have arranged to have him fired if he had of done so, this Boss of mine was a very unusual person, one who I will never forget.

On an occasional weekend, I would leave our son with my Mother and go on a trip with Bob. I guess I cramped his style for a while. My last trip with him was very scary. He was loaded with pipes that were secured by large chains. On a hillside, which was very steep and about ten or so blocks almost straight down, the brakes gave out. The truck picked up speed that was unbelievable, I yelled at Bob to gear down, he did that and stripped each gear right down to the reverse. When he applied that gear, we were at the bottom of the hill and had finally come to a full stop. Actually we were happy to find we were in one piece.

The firm sent out another truck to unload and a tow truck to bring us back home. Well at least he did not freeze with fear that time. It was after that experience that I decided that there was not going to be anymore truck rides for me. I was the one who was the chicken this time; just thought it was a good idea at the time anyway, don't you? My imagination was working overtime and I could see that load of pipes snapping and coming forward on us, bye! Yes I do know that the chains are secured and all that, but the chain is also only as good as its weakest link. That was what was going through my mind at the time.

While we were living in that house, I decided that we should have boarders as it had four bedrooms with a bath upstairs. We had one bedroom with a bath downstairs, a very large kitchen and a living-dining room area. Our babysitter stayed in a room that was in the basement which also had a separate bathroom, she liked that room the most. I went out and purchased four used bedroom suites along with new mattresses and box springs. After that I put an advertisement in the newspaper for boarders. There were four young men who answered the ad, two were university students and the two others were on their very first jobs, they were all very well behaved and quiet.

They would have breakfast and supper with us and took box lunches with them for their noon meal. It was kind of hectic at times, with holding down a full time job, cooking and cleaning for a houseful of people. Taking care of our son as well, turned out to be a real challenge for me. Everything had to be planned out carefully or I would run into trouble, time was always of the essence in these circumstances. I did not think that I was such a good cook but believe it or not, my boarders thought it was good and rarely left much on their plates. Also tried to make the meals as different as possible every day, variety is the spice of life, this also included deserts. The young men always paid on time and life seemed pretty good, it also made it easier on us financially. This was especially true for Bob as I did not find any time to keep track of him. This did last quite a while, at least a year before things started to change. It was good while it lasted and it sure lulled me into being comfortable and worry free.

Let me tell you, when I did find out about his fooling around, he did not like it very much. He beat me up so bad that I could not go to work for a while. Our tenants did not like Bob and became very protective of me at first. All together they had witnessed at least three different physical beatings and I cannot remember how many verbal lashings I received.

After a while, the young men just got fed up with it all and decided to find other homes to get away from the situation. I did not blame them one bit as they did not need to stay and put up with it; they were not married to it. Of course it was always my fault according to Bob, never was he ever wrong in his eyes. It is just awful when one takes a beating because they find out that their mate is fooling around. The irony was, that I had found out by accident; I was not looking for trouble.

The only part that was my fault was that I should

have left him and pressed charges. Another problem was that I was afraid then as the police never protected the abused at that time, they never even recognized the situation in our laws. To top it, there was absolutely no place for me to go as by then my Mother was taking care of my Grandmother. Small children make too much noise and it would only bother her. My Boss made sure that Bob no longer was employed, all that did was make him even angrier and aggressive, received another beating for that.

One day I had received notice that our rent cheque had bounced; there was not enough money in our joint account to cover the rent or utilities they all bounced. At that time it cost $5.00 per bounced cheque, it just was not easy to cover. When I asked Bob what had happened, he said that he had purchased a copper picture of a three master sailing ship in silhouette. He just had to have it, it cost him over $700.00 and it could not be returned. I hated that picture with all my heart; we just could not afford it. The picture was absolutely beautiful but it only caused me much pain, I could not love it. I eventually gave it away just so it would not remind me of the past.

At that time I was making only $100.00 per month, all the little savings from having boarders were gone. Extra money was needed to cover the expense of the bounced cheques. I went to my Boss and borrowed from him what was needed; fortunately he let me have it. He deducted a monthly payment from my pay; this was until I had it all paid back. Like I told you, he was a one in a million type of Boss.

Anyway at that time I went to the bank and had them remove my name from the joint account; opened up a new account in my name only. At least Bob would not be able to touch that account. Also went to a firm that consolidated our indebtedness and I signed a contract to pay back what I could afford. This all infuriated Bob, for my efforts I received another beating, only this time it put me into hospital for a few days. Damage was done to my right eye, the scar tissue is still there of course, fortunately I can still see okay. When in hospital, my Mother did take Teddy and cared for him at my Grandparents home, apparently my son tried to be very quiet while there.

When I was discharged from the hospital, I looked for and found a basement apartment in North Vancouver. It had a large kitchen, a small living room and a large bedroom. Off from the apartment, there was a shower-bathroom. Foolish me, a real glutton for punishment, I listened to Bob when he begged me to take him back. He promised me that he would never hit me again, you know, the same old story, BIG mistake.

For a little while, Bob actually behaved himself which lulled me once again into a serene and secure feeling. I had stopped shaking in fear, should have known though, this was not going to last. "Leopards" do not change their spots.

One day Bob purchased an old car for $100.00 and it did actually work for a while, noisy as the devil himself. Until the drive shaft cracked, it did real well, guess it just got overheated. Bob went to different scrap yards that carried old car parts and found a drive shaft that would fit the car for only $10.00. I tried to help him put it in the car but not without a lot of trouble from him. He was trying to put it in backwards and it just would not fit, logic says to turn it around and try it that way. Well smart little me again with my logic said: "Why not turn it around and see if it will fit then?" Logic always did get me into trouble, it still does cause me a lot of trouble and it sure did that time. That only made Bob angry and he would not listen to me, of course I got angry right back because he was yelling at me. How dare I challenge his knowledge on what he was doing, what does a stupid "Bitch" like me know?

Well I left him to his problem and went back in to the apartment and washed up, changed my clothes into something nice and clean. While I was doing that, Bob had decided to do what I had suggested in the first place, it worked. That did not make any difference to him; he stormed back into the apartment, full of anger, and started to knock me around again. Believe it or not, instead of fear, he infuriated me. Reason, he had made a mess of my clean clothes again, I fought back. When he went to punch me, I grabbed his fist, twisted it around to his back and shoved him into the living room, he landed on the floor. He rose up and tried again, this time I grabbed his fist and pushed him back down over the arm rest of the couch. That was when I realized that I was so angry that all of my strength was there, I could have broken his back, this I did not want. I decided instead to get his promise once more, never to try and hit me again. The promise was made and to my surprise he left us and never returned; the situation must have scared him off. I never thought I had enough strength to do what I did and know that I have not that strength today.

Chapter Five
--34--

About six months after Bob had left, our son Ted
became very ill and had pneumonia, with a high
temperature of 102.5 degrees. I gave him aspirin and
rubbed him down with Vicks, nothing helped. Well I
must tell you that, I was ever so worried about him that
I bundled him up, put him into the car, and drove him
to a hospital in Vancouver. I was afraid all the way
there and all the way back, why? Number one, the car
had no license plates and number two, all I had was a
learners' license to drive. What are the odds of not
being stopped by the police that day? Let me say that
not only was I not stopped either way, I never even saw
a Police cruiser anywhere.

Teddy was admitted to hospital and was there for
ten days before I could take him home again. I have
never driven a car since then; it really did not matter to
me at all. I have always been a "Go by Bus" type of
person, come to think of it; I would go by bus or cab to
and from everywhere. All that mattered to me at that
time was to get my son some good medical care.

When Teddy was better, I was able to take care of
the other situation, namely Bob. I hired a private
detective to find him as I knew he would be with
another foolish and beautiful female, he always needed
support from one, just too lazy that is all. It took
another year before grounds for divorce was obtained.
He was living in a bachelor suite with a young girl; this
was in Prince Rupert, B.C.

It was shortly after that, that I met my future husband. When I had to go to Prince Rupert to get my divorce, my future husband went with me so that I would not be alone. We stayed in separate rooms so as not to get into trouble at the divorce hearing; it was not that hard really. As it turned out, there was a murder trial going on in the same court room, they only had one court room in Prince Rupert. My divorce date was put on hold until the murder trial was over.

It was a very small town, not much to do at all. There was a pool hall, movie theatre, bowling alley with ten lanes and a lot of old hotels with beer parlours where you could get drunk. We went bowling a few times, took in a couple of movies and actually walked around a lot; it was quite beautiful, all old fashioned of course. Probably it is much larger and more modern today; I would like to see it again some day. That was in the year 1957, over forty-eight years ago, it has to have changed by now, right?

Finally the murder trial was over, they told me the man was convicted of killing his wife's lover; he apparently never touched her though. I went to court; the divorce trial took very little time at all. I was granted the Decree Absolute but for some reason, my lawyer had neglected to sue for full custody and child support for Teddy. After I was granted the divorce, my future husband and I returned to the hotel room and celebrated with a bottle of Danish red wine. I drank it like it was soda pop, needless to say, I did get drunk very fast and equally as fast I became very ill, boy was that ever a lesson and a half. Jim, my future husband, ordered two pots of black coffee to sober me up, all that did was make me even sicker. Eventually I started to feel better, not so dizzy and nauseous. We went for a long walk; the fresh air was the best medicine for me. That night, I slept like a baby, do not think I ever slept that good again, at least, I cannot remember doing so.

The next morning, we flew back to Vancouver; it was a good trip home. While away, my Mother took care of Teddy, she did a very good job of it too. Teddy was real happy to see his Mommy. About six months after that, I had to go to the Vancouver Court House to get custody and child support. I received full custody with no problem but the support for Teddy was only $20.00 per month, ridiculous right? That turned out to be a "Catch me if you can" proposition as Bob was rarely working, he was once again being supported by a woman. Sometimes we women never learn but that is life. What attracted me to him in the first place, I will never know, oh foolish heart.

All during this time period, I paid my Boss back for what he loaned me and also all of the other indebtedness, it had taken time but now it was finished. Thought that I would look for other employment in North Vancouver instead of travelling so far by bus, I was successful at that and would start in three weeks time. Doing it this way enabled me to give plenty of notice to my old job and receive a good reference besides. I started work for a small place in North Vancouver, just wonder if it is still there or have they ceased to exist. Maybe they have even changed their name, a lot of businesses have. It was a good place to work and really enjoyed the time there. Anyway there were specific jobs for me to do; it never did keep me busy. It took only the last few days and the first few days of the month, that was the extent of my work. It was not long before I went looking for more to do and, ended up helping everyone in all departments including the Big Boss. By doing it this way, I found that it kept me constantly busy, with helping everyone, no one ever got behind in their work. With computers now they are set up differently, cannot see it being the same.

While there, my Boss made sure that I had all the latest technical equipment to work with. He purchased an electric typewriter and calculator for me, in those days the top quality was the Olivetti machines. I did become very good at using these machines, and still am pretty good with the figures and typing. Oh yes, I also had the latest in dictating machines of that time, really did love my work. At times it became quite demanding after I went hunting for more to do, truly did have an enjoyable job. There was never another job like it or as enjoyable as it was.

Even at this time, I was having a great difficulty

coping with what I had been through and was still going through, became quite bitter for a while. Unfortunately you had to solve all of your own problems; there were no support vehicles then. It was really hard to do it by oneself and know what was right. The one thing I did not want; was to become like my Mother all the rest of my life, bitter.

One day my Husband-to-be took me on a movie date, it was a movie called "I Don't Want to Die," this was quite a brutal picture. The story was about a married woman who was an alcoholic; she was used and abused by her husband and others. At one time in the movie, she was under the influence of both alcohol and drugs, in other words, in a real stupor. Her husband and friends were at their place partying it up. When she woke up, she was alone with a dead body. She was charged, convicted of murder and sentenced to die in the electric chair.

It was just before the execution that her husband came to visit. He told her that he had framed her and that it was actually him that had murdered the person she was convicted of. All through that movie, the woman was bitter and angry with good cause of course; I could see myself in her. I sincerely thought that it was a story of fiction. After that, I had decided that I was going to straighten myself out and not blame others for what had happened. In my grim determination, it worked; I soon ceased my bitterness. Determination goes a long way, and everyone can find happiness, whether it is with children, adults or seniors. Even working with animals or just having pets can help you cope with the bitterness you feel. There is the warmth, love and loyalty that you receive unconditionally.

Sometime later I went shopping for patterns, fabrics and trims, did some pinning and cutting out of the patterns. I then sat down at the old treadle Singer sewing machine of my Mothers' and made myself some lovely new clothes. My future husband sat down with me and watched me sew. This turned out to be my therapy for all my problems and it really did work, see, we can help ourselves. When I tried on each outfit that I had made, Jim complimented me on how I looked, did not look too bad at all, if I do say so myself. Jim purchased a string of pearls and a set of earrings to match; this was for me to wear with my ice blue satin dress and bolero jacket. The outfit really turned out beautiful and matched my blue eyes.

At that same time, I also made myself a beautiful sheer white silk dress that was embroidered with little white flowers, lined it with white taffeta which made it rustle as I moved. It had an empire bodice, sleeveless, a slender waist with eight panels in the front and back of the skirt. To go with the dress I also made a multilayered crinoline petticoat to wear underneath it. This made the dress stand right out; it also suited me and turned out like I never thought that it would, just breathtaking. Jim purchased a set of earrings and a necklace made of gold aurora borealis stones to go with the dress. Along with the dress, jewellery and new hairdo I wore a pair of white sling back high heeled shoes; this was all touched off with a deep purple orchid corsage.

We went out to bring in the New Year in Chinatown, Vancouver. Jim wore a very smart black suit with a white boutonniere, white shirt and a purple tie, he looked really good. He put on a Texas Drawl and pretended to be a Texas Oil Baron, the irony was everyone who was there believed him. It was all put on to impress me, well it did and I admit it.

At midnight, when the fireworks went off, Jim picked me up and put me on the table. This was so that I could watch the fireworks from a better place; of course one of my shoes fell off. Just like in Cinderella and Prince Charming, he sat me down, went down on one knee and put my shoe back on. That was truly a wonderful evening all round, flattering in every way, lovely and completely unforgettable. We never had another New Years like that, we just could not afford it, no matter; it is a great memory in my memory bank. Everyone should have an experience like that at least once in their lifetime, a Fairy Tale come true.

Approximately six months later, Jim proposed to me, of course I said yes. We went ring hunting and found just what we wanted, a lovely pair of rings for me and a really nice wedding band for him. It was on one of those searches that we came across my Father and his wife Patricia. It was the first time in years since I had seen them. My Father put his hand on my shoulder and Jim was going to hit him, I said: "No-no it is my Dad." What a way to meet his future Father-in-law, we did have a nice long conversation though and found out that there were more children.

The last time I visited with my Father, there were five children, the eldest being Joseph, who did not like me, he only tolerated me. Then there was Mary, the eldest girl, she became closest to me, we loved each other instantly. The next child was Shirley, a blonde, she was not too sure of me at all. Found out later that she was in awe of me and that was why she kept her distance from me. After that Elizabeth came to being, whom I absolutely adore and finally there was John. He was the youngest at that time and I have not seen him since.

Maybe I have someone in reverse order, I hope not. My brother Bill came later, I finally met him in the summer of 2005. Steve was next, whom I have great rapport with, also love so very much. Irene was next in line and whom I absolutely adore, she is super special. I have since found out that we have a lot in common. She was born in 1954, the same year as my son Ted. June was the last girl and I have never met her. Lastly there was Eddy whom I met when he was just sixteen years of age.

Eddy was the one who gave me a bit of a bad time, since then, he has turned out to be a super person. I am truly pleased with him as he has done really well for himself, am proud of all his accomplishments. Once again, I pray that everyone is in the right order, if not I hope they forgive me. Want everyone to know, though we have different Mothers, I consider all of them as my full blooded Sisters and Brothers. Whether they love me or not, my love for them will always be there, they are all special to me.

Chapter Six

--43--

Jim and I decided that our Wedding Day would be December 24th. 1959 and that it would be in a Chapel of a United Church in North Vancouver. We would have only immediate family members in attendance and the reception would be at Jim's Parent's home. For the wedding, I made my Mother a salmon coloured dress that was embossed with tiny flowers. For my to-be-Sister-in-law, I made a fitted dress which she absolutely adored and lost weight for. For the flower girl, I made a dress in a soft orange, full skirted with a multi-layered crinoline. So that her sister would not feel left out, I had made her a matching dress.

For myself I made a dress that was in a very turquoise taffeta that shimmered in the lights, it had a full paneled skirt, empire bodice with short sleeves, including a multi-layered crinoline. I later purchased turquoise netting and made a wide brimmed hat and elbow length gloves to go with my dress. My white sling back shoes were dyed to match, they were beautifully done.

For Teddy who was the ring bearer, I made a black suit; with it he wore a white shirt and black tie. In the pocket there was a white handkerchief just like Jims. The groom wore a black suit, white shirt, black tie, white handkerchief and a white boutonniere, so did my cousin Fred who was our Best Man. Both Jim and Fred looked great and in miniature so did Teddy.

For the Bridal flowers, I held an imitation white satin Bible with a white gardenia corsage on top. It had white ribbon streamers with flower buds on the end of each ribbon falling from it. Each of attendants had a wrist corsage with the same flower and the flower girl also had a basket of pink and white flower petals. My Uncle Mike was our Chauffeur and he did an excellent job of it, he made us feel like royalty, what an Uncle, just super.

Jim spent the day cooking our reception meal of ham, roast beef, gravy, and baked potatoes, mixed vegetables, and tossed salad. For dessert, we had plum pudding with ice cream and lastly a piece of Wedding Cake. While he was doing the cooking, I was running around picking up everything that was previously ordered, including the Wedding Cake. To my amazement I had returned with the cake in good order, nothing broken, also picked up my shoes and Jim's suit pants. The reason for the suit pants was because they had to be altered as Jim had lost too much weight and he would have looked sloppy if not done. This I did by bus not by cab or car, pretty good job I think.

After our guests left, we went to bed and was almost driven nuts by a ticking sound. We looked everywhere in the room and never found it until we looked between the mattress and the box spring. When we did that, we found our alarm clock which my Aunt Agnes had hidden. This Aunt was always playing tricks on people; this was our turn to be on the receiving end of her pranks. She thought doing this would make the beginning of our marriage a little more interesting. The thing is, we never noticed or missed her when she had decided to lay this trap for us. She did start our marriage off with a little more excitement. Have often wondered what she did at her sons Weddings, knowing my aunt, she would have done something to put a buzz into things.

Before we got married, Jim's work told him that he had to transfer to Winnipeg, Manitoba or not have a job to go to. Of course we decided together, that we would make the move, no question about it. It seemed a little scary to me at first but, I am game to try just about anything. When we made plans for our Wedding we also made arrangements to move and travel by train to Winnipeg. We were on a train pass and it would cost us only for our meals and extra coffee if we wanted it.

The day after our Wedding, I made us Christmas dinner of stuffed turkey, gravy, mashed potatoes, corn, tossed salad and plum pudding with almond sauce. It was the noon meal for us and it turned out lovely, felt really great about myself that day. For dinner we went downstairs to Jim's Parent's suite. There was stuffed turkey, mashed potatoes, gravy, cabbage rolls, pirogues, (potato and cheddar cheese type), borscht (beet soup) with sour cream. It was all topped off with coffee and Christmas cake and ice cream. With our meal upstairs we had wine and downstairs we had rum and coke. This mixture set me up for getting really ill, I just was no drinker.

When I woke up on Boxing Day, I was sick from the liquor that I had consumed the day before. With a headache and nausea, eating was not an option for me. Of course we had to pack up all our belongings to be picked up by truck that night. Since I could not do a thing, Jim did all the packing and took care of Teddy too. He packed only what we would need for the seven days as our possessions would arrive by then.

Jim, Teddy and I caught the train the morning of December 28th. It was a completely new experience for Teddy and myself; not complaints, it was a great ride. If you wish to travel a scenic route, go by train, it is just fabulous.

When we arrived in Winnipeg, it was beastly cold and a lot of new snow on the ground. We were met by Jim's long time friend, Wally; he took us to his home where we stayed until we found our own place to live. We also went to the Credit Union to arrange for a loan to start us out, we were flat broke. We found an apartment right next door to where we were staying, it was also reasonable on the rent.

The Railroad then sent Jim on the road again, leaving me to wait for our possessions to arrive; they did on the second of January 1960. Wally helped me move everything around and set-up the television, the rest I did myself. Really felt great about doing it all, it was all put away nice and neat, even had the telephone hooked up. Let me say that winter was the hardest on me. I wore two pair of long cotton stockings, two pairs of Jim's long johns, and his heavy work socks. On the outside, I wore a pair of sweat bottoms and tops, a couple of sweaters, a parka, a scarf and a pair of heavy duty mitts. Even at that I still shivered; I will never forget that winter.

The next winter I was fully acclimatized and never had to wear so much again. Even now I dress pretty light for an old gal, correction, I do not feel old so I had better not use the word right? When Jim came home off the road, we went house hunting and found this place; it is now over 100 years old. It cost us $970.00 mortgage, and $10.00 in coins down payment. We had to borrow a couple of thousand dollars to renovate, get a new furnace and hot water tank. We took possession on May 1st. 1960, we never moved to any other place after that.

Jim's brother Peter helped us to move to this house, he was supposed to be a professional mover, ha-ha; no one can make me believe that. He managed to break the freezer door, our television and the record player. Everything was repaired over time except for the freezer door. It was a heck of a way to meet one's brother-in-law.

About ten days after we moved in, a friend of Jim's asked him if he would like to adopt a child. If yes, we had to get our Doctor to take care of the Mother-to-be, we had to let him know right away. We did say yes and made an appointment with our new Doctor for her. It cost us $10.00 per month for her care until it was all paid off, our Doctor did a good job for her. He also arranged for the adoption papers to be drawn up.

The baby was born on June 19th.1960 and we received a phone call from the birth Mother telling us she had a little boy. He weighed in at 5 pounds 6 ½ ounces; he was 23 inches long, very tiny. She asked if we wanted him to be circumcised and I said absolutely, yes. She had changed her mind back and forth several times and almost drove me crazy over the last month before the birth. We had made arrangements to meet in the restaurant across the street from the hospital. When Daniel was only six days old, I received him from the birth Mother. I was very excited; the only thing that I was afraid of is she might change her mind again. It was then that I sent Jim a wire announcing to him that he was a Father of a brand new baby boy.

When we met Jim at the train station, he took one look at Daniel and said: "He's an ugly looking little bugger isn't he?" I told him that he was not ugly; he was just wrinkled like a little old man and had a case of cradle cap. All new born babies are like that and in all cases they change in a short period of time; Daniel's did clear up.

It did not take long for Jim to love and cuddle him. He just would not change diapers; he said that is the Mother's job.

On our first visit to the Doctors, he told us that Daniel had FAS (Fetal Alcohol Syndrome). The child will have very little feelings; also he will have great difficulty in learning; we were not to expect too much of Daniel. We did not care as he needed love, a home and family like every other child does. We did the very best we could for him; he has often told me how glad he is that we adopted him.

Daniel has seen many other children like himself not have someone to care for them and help out when they needed assistance. Most of them ended up in prison or on the street with nothing. He does care what has happened to him and tries very hard to show this in all that he does. I am not in the least disappointed in Daniel.

When Jim went back on the road, I had two to care for; no time to feel sorry for myself. It was during that period of time that I did all the washing the old fashioned way, yup, you guessed it. It was the old scrubbing board; it seems that I could never get away from it. This was the way until I could afford to purchase a washing machine. That would be taken care of in the very near future, not in the way that you may think.

One day I was outside working in the front yard garden when I seen a little girl with two younger siblings tagging along. Shortly after looking, the smallest child had darted out into the street, I darted right after her. Reason, was there was a car coming down the street and it was moving pretty fast. I picked the child up and fell backwards on to the boulevard; both of us were okay. I asked the eldest little girl where did they come from, she told me from the corner. Then I asked her to wait in the yard while I went inside to get my baby, I picked up Daniel and we all went to the children's home. On the way we talked, the eldest was taking care of her younger siblings and that she was only five years old. The thing that upset me as well as made me angry was she was far too young to be watching them. The boy was three years old and the little one was only two.

When we reached their home, I knocked on the door, heard "Come in," then we entered the apartment. The Mother was sitting having coffee with a neighbour, that made me even angrier. I informed her that she almost lost her youngest child, by what means and how angry this had made me. When she stood up, I saw that she was very pregnant, and I actually ended up making friends with her. I gave her my phone number and told her to call me if she ever needed any help, I would be very glad to help her out if I could. She did keep track of her little ones after that, they were not wandering around the neighbourhood without an adult escort again. I returned home with Daniel and checked on

Ted who was at another neighbour's house, seen that he was playing okay and behaving himself.

Ted started school in September 1960; he was having trouble right from the start with his learning. His teacher was very short tempered like myself; she had absolutely no patience with Ted. After I had a talk with her, she tried harder and really got along with Ted. It was that month when Jim returned home and we joined a United Church. We arranged to have both Daniel and Ted Baptized on the following Sunday, the first Sunday in November. Daniel's godparents were Jim's best friend Wally and his wife Rita; Ted's godparents were Jim's brother Peter and his wife Yvonne. It was a beautiful ceremony, I shall never forget it. Ted wore his black suit that I had made for our wedding and Daniel had a Christening gown and cap on, they looked just great

About two weeks later, the young Mother down the street went into labour and had stillborn twin sons. She ended up in hospital severely undernourished; had to be put on a high protein diet and kept there until her health improved. It was her Mother that phoned me and let me know what had happened; she gave me the phone number at the hospital. The reason that she called was the little girl who is now six years old was staying with her and she did not want to care for the child. It was then that I found out, the two youngest were in Foster care and separated from each other.

Received permission from the children's Mother to take care of the six year old as well as take in the two youngest. All three of them were turned over to me, one at a time. The Grandmother brought over the six year old, later the same day the little boy arrived. He was ever so glad to see his big sister, there was so much excitement. At around four o'clock, the youngest was brought to me; they were all squealing with delight at finding they were all together.

After all the excitement died down, I changed the two youngest diapers. The boy was just fine; he had no problems over not being changed often enough. Only the youngest girl was in dire need of care, whoever had her never changed her diaper for at least that whole day. That child had one massive urine blister on her bottom area. I reported the condition the child was in, also said that this particular foster family should not have any children in their care. Of course they told me they would take care of it, I do not know if they did. The reason I think they did not do a thing about it is that they needed foster care badly. It is hard to find families to take children in; as far as I know it is still the same way today. Nothing has changed over the years; I do know they were glad that I had taken these children into my home. It was probably the one reason that we had no trouble with our adoptions. They did see the love and care that we gave to these little ones.

The youngest child never cried when I took care of her blistered little bottom. I gently bathed and used

Zinc Oxide on her at every change, the special care allowed her skin to heal quickly. The Grandmother was the problem to me; she would try and interfere with my caring for the children. One day when she came over to take the older girl out, she did not like what I fed them. The Grandmother said that I was mean because I would not allow them to eat their dessert first. I told her this: "These children are in my care in my home, I treat them as my own, love them like my own. They will eat what we eat and when we eat it. If you do not like it, you will not be welcome here; you must go by my rules and keep quiet." Her husband was doubled over in laughter, I do not think anyone ever told her off before, do not think they dared. I dared because it was not only in my home but her daughter needed the help. There was nothing she could do about it because she could not take care of the children.

Let me say, I never regretted doing this for that family; I thoroughly enjoyed and loved her children. While with me, I kept them busy at all times and not running around the neighbourhood. Because their Mother had little financially, she gave me a bedroom suite and a wringer washer. That washing machine lasted me for years, clothes pegs held the wringers in place so that I could use them. It was old and truly done for by the time I bought a new one, the new one was one of a pair washer/dryer, what a difference.

Our first Christmas in this house was just glorious; I made most of the decorations from hangers and tin foil. Covered part of the tin foil with plastic flowers bought from a craft store and added ribbon and one tree bauble, they lasted for thirty years before falling apart. Also made Christmas tree decorations by cutting out Santa's, Angels and bells, made streamers from popcorn, they had to be made yearly. While we were putting up our tree, we talked about taking a trip to Vancouver, we both missed our families. We made our reservations to go by train; Ted had a ball with the variety of people on board. Daniel was too small to care one way or another; we were looking forward to showing him off to our families. We had phoned Jim's Mother so that she would know when we were coming. Jim's Sister picked us up and drove us to his Mother's home; we truly enjoyed seeing them again.

The day after our arrival, we went to see my Mother, she was very glad to see us and her brand new Grandchild. We spent the day with her and told her she was going to spend Christmas day at Jim's Mother's home and she agreed to it. We went to my Aunt and Uncles home the following day, we had a marvellous time with them and their family, it was a wonderful experience. The next day, my Uncle Mike picked us up and drove us to visit with my Grandmother. She was absolutely thrilled when she saw us and her newest Great-Grandson. I was surprised that she had lost both of her legs through gangrene. I knew she was a diabetic but it still was a shock to me to see her in that shape. Apparently, after losing her second leg, her diabetes turned to a type two, it had surprised her Doctors and they could not explain why this happened to her.

While in Vancouver, we visited with many of our other friends and family that we had not seen for a long time. We had a lovely Ukrainian Christmas dinner with Jim's family, my Mother thoroughly enjoyed the visit with them. Another thing; she received the opportunity to speak her own language once more, just never had much chance to use it over the years.

When we returned to Winnipeg, Ted opened his presents. There were toy trucks, cars and a hooded parka that I had made for him. I also made two shirts that were a complete match for both Jim and Ted. Those shirts lasted a long time, as a matter of fact; they were handed down until they fell apart. Daniel received a few stuffed toys from Santa; he played with them as babies do.

In January, Ted returned to school and had trouble adjusting to a strict behavioural condition again. That was when we decided that we were not going to take any trips during a school term; Ted only rebelled when he returned to school. As a matter of fact, Ted was so stubborn and so was his teacher; that his class room was in total chaos at times. The teacher decided right then that Ted was incorrigible instead of trying to find a way to help him. How can a six year old be incorrigible? Well it is possible, but no one, not even us knew what the problem was at that time. It was quite a few years before it was diagnosed, it never improved; it only got worse over time. All the way through school it was a struggle, Teddy thought he had to compete with me, this I did not understand.

There were times that Teddy would take Daniel's bottle or his soother, just to make him cry. Sometimes he would ditch the soother down the hot air vent or in the garbage. No matter how I tried to incorporate Teddy into helping with Daniel; Teddy would find a way to rebel. Then again, there were a few times when he actually co-operated and did help me. It was then that I would give him a compliment on a job well done and a hug and a kiss to prove it. We were beginning to think that he was too old for younger children, of course that was not true, it just seemed that way. Jim and I talked a lot about it and decided we would try to adopt another child if we ever received the opportunity. We were not lucky enough to produce our own; maybe it was a good thing as between us there were too many health problems in later life. The one thing we did not want was too many years between Daniel and the next child, no more rebellions between the children.

Somewhere in this time period, Daniel was crawling around and he found my pot cupboard, what a noisy time that was. He would squeal with delight over the racket they made. He amused himself completely different than most other children did, Daniel just did not like to play with others.

In September 1961 my Husband was not feeling very well in his tummy, I made an appointment for him to see the Doctor. When on the examining table the Doctor pressed down on his tummy and made him holler. At the same time as he was doing this he asked Jim: "How would you like to adopt another child?" Needless to say he said yes but had to ask me if I wanted to do so, I would have to call the Doctor and let him know.

When I called the Doctor back, he told me that the child was a result of a couple's infidelity to each other. They wanted to try and make a go of their marriage so needed to put the coming birth up for adoption. Their religion does not believe in divorce or abortion, it was absolutely out of the question for them. Keeping the child was also out of the question as it would have been a constant reminder of their own shortcomings. They would not be able to live with themselves if they had agreed to an abortion. All I can say is thank GOD, because my beautiful Son would never have been born. I probably would never have had such a good friend in him, for this I am truly thankful.

The baby was due in late January or early February. We were excited and thought that just maybe; the little one would arrive on Jim's birthday, February 7th. 1962. The only thing that we had to make sure of was not to allow them to baptize the baby. If they baptized the baby, the child would never be ours, that is one rule of their religion and it cannot be broken.

Come January 19th. 1962 we were downtown to sign the final adoption papers for Daniel and the Mother's own adoption of Teddy. Teddy's new name was Ted James and the baby's name was Daniel Trent. When we arrived home, there was a little elderly man on a bicycle waiting for us with a note from our Doctor. We were proud parents of a new baby boy once again, he weighed in at 8 pounds, 15 ounces and 28 inches long, big baby. The reason he was born early, apparently the birth Mother came down with a very bad cold. This brought on the birth of the child, no matter though, we had our little boy.

There was only nineteen months between our new baby and Daniel, no rebellions and it was just super. Anyway the Doctor had tried to call us; of course we were out taking care of the adoption papers as it was equal in importance. I had to call our Doctor and let him know that we wanted our new baby circumcised. He was named Fredrick Alexander after a Great Grandfather and a Great-Great Grandfather on Jim's side.

We did have one problem though; the hospital contacted us and informed us that the other religious group wanted to baptize our little one. I phoned our lawyer first and he would not do a thing about it as he too was of that religion. That same lawyer had decided that he did not want to help us; we ended up letting him go and later hired another. We then contacted our Doctor and along with the birth parents assistance settled the matter really quick. After five days, our friend Rita and our Doctor brought our little one home; Rita was carrying the baby. Our Doctor had his pockets full of formula and the recipe for same. Of course I noticed right off that Fredrick had blue eyes not brown. The Doctor said: "Give it time, they will change to brown." I did notice his eyes changed slowly to brown over the next few months, it was quite a sight. I did not know that this process usually happened to brown eyed babies, we learn something new everyday.

When Fredrick was home only one week we had him baptized in our Church. This was because I did not trust the other religion and wanted no surprises. His Godparents were Anita and Kerry; yes they were the couple from down the street. They only had one worry, how much of an obligation it would be for them. We informed them that their only obligation was what they wished it to be. There was a time, long ago, when it was an obligation when something happened to the parents, not anymore. That Sunday, wouldn't you know it, we were having a blizzard. That did not matter to any of us; the Baptism took place as we wanted it to. Well once again, it was a very emotional ceremony for me. It was just beautiful and I will never forget it.

After the first few days Fredrick would keep me up all night rocking and singing to him. As it turned out, he had colic. The Doctor put him on a green syrupy medication. It took over a month before there was relief for Fredrick, in total; it was forty-two nights in a row that he cried. Once it took effect, there was peace in the house again, no more painful tummy. During that bad period, whenever Jim came home off the road, he would take care of Fredrick just so that I could get some rest. We both were glad when the problem ceased.

One morning when I was giving Fredrick his bath he christened his Daddy. By that I mean, he peed right over his head and got both himself and Jim, they hollered in unison. I still laugh when I think of it; both Fredrick and Daniel did that to their Daddy.

Fredrick had very sensitive skin so I never could use plastic anywhere on his bottom. If I ever did, he would become absolutely raw, this was no good. He was a little rascal though, had pixie eyes, always shining and full of mischief. He loved to go around the house naked and never hesitated to drop his diaper anywhere then laugh like crazy. He was such a happy child, unlike Daniel; Fredrick was noisy all the time.

When we would go to bed, Fredrick would peek at us and laugh, that had to stop, what we needed was a little privacy. Because of this, we moved him into the same bedroom as Daniel; they had a ball together every night. Fredrick was a rocker and he would often block the bedroom doorway with his crib. Jim took off the castors and reinforced the crib with 2x3 inch cross beams, it was necessary or the crib would not last. Believe it or not it worked; this did help keep the crib from falling apart. It did not stop Fredrick from rocking; he eventually grew out of it when he graduated to a bed.

Both Daniel and Fredrick were very close when small and still are in many ways. Daniel was the one who trained Fredrick to use the toilet when he needed to go. You know, it was marvellous to have one teach the other, Daniel did an excellent job. If anyone would have told me how much I would and could love my two sons, I would not have believed them. My sons are ever so precious to me and have never regretted adopting them, they are my life. I know it is "God's" Principle not to have pride but, I am filled with love and pride for both of my sons, they are and will forever be in my heart.

Our third Christmas was truly a wonderful one. We gave Ted a hockey game; some new clothes as well as quite a few stocking stuffers, toy trucks, candies, nuts and mandarin oranges. Daniel received fifteen dinky toys; it was a complete set of farm implements. Fredrick received a lot of stuffed toys that he absolutely loved; especially throwing them at Daniel. One of his stuffed toys had a squeaker in it; he would squeeze it just to hear it make a noise. That was the year that I had joined the Church Choir, it was something that I truly enjoyed with all my heart. This gave me the opportunity to express my love of God through song, the joy and satisfaction was tremendous. It was the year where the Choir travelled to different senior residences and nursing homes, the joy we gave with our singing was just beautiful.

When Fredrick discovered his voice, peace was out of the question after that. Fredrick's first word was Dadda, it was the exact opposite of Daniel; his first word was Momma. Once Fredrick started pulling himself around on the furniture, he was into everything; nothing stopped him from that day forward.

Believe it or not, Daniel played many hours every day with his little brother. This only reinforced our belief that we did the right thing in adopting both of them so close together. There was no rebellion between the two of them like there was between Ted and Daniel. Of course Fredrick had no concept on what was different in Daniel like Ted did, he accepted his brothers without a problem. Ted would only accept what was perfect in his eyes, in reality there is no such thing as perfect. Ted could never see himself at all; he thought he was the smartest and the best in the family. As a prime example, Ted was having a lot of problems with his school work at that time. I assisted as much as

Ted needed me to, there were times it was real difficult, but we worked out everything with his teachers. A lot of his school projects Ted enjoyed tremendously and so did I. That is probably where I received most of my education, through my sons. We still did not know what was wrong with Ted; it really left us shaking our heads.

Come summer time, we made arrangements to go on holiday to Vancouver. It was an exciting trip, thank goodness for the train pass, without it we would never have gone anywhere. All the way to Vancouver, Ted had begged food off other passengers even though we told him not to, he did not listen. Of course what they gave him was food he was not used to, it made him very ill. Jim had to take care of him as I had my hands full with our two little ones; it was one trip that Ted never forgot.

When we arrived in Jasper, which by the way is a truly a beautiful place, Jim wanted to get off and get ice cream for everyone. I did not want to get off because I was afraid we would miss getting back on the train and be stranded. How foolish I was, we would not have missed it because firstly we had plenty of time and secondly the ice cream parlours were close to the train. As it turned out, it was terribly hot and humid that day. If I had of gone out, my asthma would have kicked in and would have made me very ill. Heat and humidity just does not mix well with me, oh well, that is life.

When we were going through Kelowna, B.C., it was just after a rain fall. That was when I saw the mountain side, it was absolutely gorgeous, I swore that one day I would put it on canvas in a painting. Yes, that is another thing that I just love to do is paint. That mountain woke up my love of art; it was multi-coloured. The colours were all pastel pinks, blues, greens, yellows and mauves, all iridescent in their shades, too beautiful to describe.

We stayed at my sister-in-laws place in North Vancouver, the boys had an absolute ball. There was a large swimming pool and a lot of brambles; of course our little Fredrick managed to get himself tangled in them. We had to pull a lot of sharp needles out of his soft skin; he survived the ordeal. It was not without crying though, I am sure that those bramble needles hurt like the devil.

This trip was truly great; I played bingo with my Mother-in-law and Sister-in-law at a Church hall in Vancouver. We went out quite a few times, never won a single thing but that was no surprise to me. Jim and our Brother-in-law went to play darts on the same evenings at the Legion Hall, they really did enjoy themselves. Jim bought himself a set of heavy darts and a lighter set for me. Yes I did get to go with them a few times, even won a couple of games, not too bad for a greenhorn. It is a true game of skill and you must have excellent eyesight. If you do not have very good eyes, you will never gauge the distance to the dart board correctly. Just take my word for it if you cannot hit the board, your eyes are bad.

While there I made it a rule that I would only play bingo when in Vancouver as you can get carried away with it. Like every other gambling game, I was very careful not to go over the limit I had set myself. This was a must because extra funds I did not have and winning was a rare option. With Lotto, I play it only when it is between the 10 to 20 million jackpot sizes. The reason for this is I found that it can run into too much money. My minimum amount is $3.00 and the maximum amount is $5.00, this way I still have a chance at a win and not have an empty pocket book. If you do not play at least that amount, you do not have a chance at all. If I ever was lucky enough to win, I believe that it would knock me on my backside with shock. Also for me, the only way that I receive money is to earn it; just jinxed I guess. Then again, when do you get something for nothing?

While we were at my Sister-in-laws, I was not feeling too well one day so decided to have a lay down in our room. I woke up to the bed moving, it was our little niece who had crawled up on the bed and she opened the window beside me. Apparently that window was not locked and I did not know that. I grabbed hold of her as she started to fall, let me tell you, that scared me and my heart rate went up. She did not fall and I locked that window immediately. All I can say is that I am glad that I was there or she would have fallen two and a half stories to the concrete below. No doubt about it, she would have been seriously injured, if not killed outright. Those windows remained locked and all my nieces are still alive and well. Thank GOD for that; it just goes to show you how very precious life really is.

We went to my Mother's house while we were there, we talked her into coming to Winnipeg with us, she agreed. We made the arrangements for her to be on the same train with us, she lived with us for a whole year. While here she found work in a furniture factory stripping paint and varnish off old pieces of furniture. My Mother actually enjoyed doing this but I am afraid that it was that place along with her chain smoking that finished her life. I could not take the place at all; we made plans to have lunch together one day, I walked in and immediately left. The polluted air took my breath away; it had made me ill for a couple of days. Asthma does not like strong odours, how could my Mother take it?

While my Mother was with us I thought that maybe I could return to school to become a Certified Public Accountant. With me numbers were a love; I was a perfectionist when it came to them. When I asked my Husband, of course the answer was no, he said that I belonged at home with our children. There was no doubt about it; my children did need me so I believe Jim was right at that time. It would have been great for me if it was possible for me to have returned to school, I just could not be selfish about it though.

During this time, my Husband was on the road a lot and when he was not, he would get into arguments with my Mother. It was hell for me because they both used me in the middle and I felt like I was walking on eggshells. Not to mention it also played hell on the boys, it was not good for them to see and hear that, actually it was down right heartbreaking.

In August 1964, my Husband had a real bad argument with my Mother and I asked him to apologize, he said he would not. I told him that my Mother was ill and he would regret that decision. She just was not walking right, I could not explain what I meant by saying that, it just was. Her room smelled of death and to me, something was definitely wrong with her, Jim chose not to believe me.

My Husband went back on the road again. As it turned out, after he left, my Mother complained of so much pain that I gave her a bath and took her to hospital. It was during this bath that if I touched her she would cry out because her skin was so sore. At the base of her head at the back are lymph nodes, there were two lumps the size of robins' eggs; this told me that she was dying of cancer.

I took my children to my next door neighbour's house and then took my Mother to hospital; she was admitted that same day. Thank GOD for good and dear neighbours, they allowed me to stay with my Mother as long as I needed to. When I returned home,

I phoned my Husband and told him what I found on my Mother. Also told him that it was my impression that she had cancer and would not live long, he was amazed and said so.

I had prayed to GOD that he would not let my Mother suffer anymore, He did that for me; she went into a coma that night. When I went to the hospital they did not want me to touch her as it would set off the machines that were attached to her. I pleaded with them to at least let me hold her hand as she was not going to be here much longer. Of course they told me that I did not know what I was talking about. I may not have been a nurse but I have learned from every experience and knew that I was right. When I returned home that night, after feeding and putting the boys to bed, I sat down and wrote a letter. It was to my Sister-in-law in North Vancouver, she was very pregnant at the time. While sitting in my rocking chair, I took note of the time and wrote it down in the letter. It was 4:17 a.m. and I wrote that my Mother had just passed away, I was not aware that I had done this. It was when she called me on the phone that she told me what I had written the day my Mother died. I had prayed to GOD that He would take her quickly and He did just that for me. I was and still am forever thankful that she did not suffer anymore.

At six a.m. that morning, the hospital phoned me to tell me that my Mother has passed away at 4:40 a.m.

I told them that it was not true; she had passed at 4:17 a.m. They asked me how I could know this, I told them that my Mother and I were very close and that she was still with me. I then phoned my Husband with the news; he came home right away and took care of all the funeral arrangements as I was in no condition to do so. The time between knowing how ill my Mother was and her passing was so short that it as a total shock to me. I am forever grateful that my Husband was able and did take care of this for me; he did a really good job. I was unable to cry until after the wake and that was when I flew off the handle because of the mess they left my house in. My Husband did regret the arguments he had with my Mother all of his life. He never apologized to her over them and she is and was the only one who could forgive him for them.

After the funeral my Husband went back on the road again and I went to see our Doctor to get something to calm me down. He put me on a tranquilizer for a long period of time. I was taking too many and our Doctor was not keeping track of my medications. One night when my Husband was off the road he went to a Union Meeting; I was feeling very depressed. Because of this, I had taken all of my tranquilizers and ended up in hospital unaware. The law said it is illegal to take ones own life; well maybe so, but what can they do about it if you are successful, put you in prison? Funny!!

I had to report to the Police upon leaving the hospital and had to see a Psychiatrist, I did both. The Psychiatrist declared me okay and told me that I would not try to do that again, he was right. I never did try to do that again, to me life is far too beautiful to give up, and GOD gave me this one. My personal Physician was angry because I was not taking anymore of his prescription and he wanted me to find another Doctor. I was so angry with him that I actually blasted him for his attitude. I told him: "It was your fault for not keeping track of my medications and that I have no intention of changing Doctors. You had better get adjusted to it as I was still not going to take anymore tranquilizers no matter what." We did make up and become friends again; he continued to be our Doctor until he was forced to retire, that was many years later. This man gave me and my whole family top notch treatment, he treated us more like family and never let us down again.

After Daniel started school, we did find help for him. In the school system there were special programs for children that had problems like him, just so that life would not be quite so hard on them. The only trouble with it at that time, it was only up to the grade seven level, not higher, that was really rough. Daniel often panicked when he just could not understand the work that they gave him. Believe me it did help me out a lot as I learned to cope with the problems that both Ted and Daniel came up with. I was not perfect but at least

I tried; I loved them both so much and still do. I would have liked it to be a wee bit easier but it was not to be so, just made the best of what I knew and had.

In the summer 1965 we went for another visit to Vancouver and found that Jim's Father was having a lot of trouble with his legs. They were going to operate on him and had asked for him to be admitted to hospital. When we went to see him after the operation, I once again could smell death, it's something you never want to experience. I knew that Jim's Father was not going to last long and we were scheduled to leave that night on the train. He had said his goodbyes to us and told me that we would not see him again, I believed him as we all know when our end is near. We boarded our train home and I told Jim that he would not get his bags unpacked before we would receive a call on Dad's passing. When we arrived in Winnipeg, sure enough when we walked in the front door, the phone did ring. It was July 23, 1965 and Jim returned to Vancouver for his Father's funeral.

That year in December, I had become ill. At first it was thought that I had kidney stones and was being treated for it. It was excruciatingly painful; no one ever would want to have a problem with the kidneys. Because of the pain my Doctor told my Husband to take me to hospital, he did just that. They took me to a special x-ray where I had to be injected with a dye. As it turned out, I was allergic to it and promptly passed out.

Of that day, I remember very little, it was night time before I came to. At that time they also told me what was wrong with me. Apparently I had three kidneys and one was bleeding into my system causing me great pain. Besides that I had an infection and had to have a lot of antibiotics to clear it up. That year I spent my birthday in hospital. Jim brought me a cyclamen plant and a large birthday cake, this I shared with everyone on the floor who could have a piece. That was one way to get some much needed rest, a nice hospital stay; at least I was able to catch up on my crocheting.

Chapter Eight

One day in the year 1966, my Husband was home on a break period; it was at the same time as the seven day war by Israel. It was at this time that I was just getting over a bad case of the flu and had sacked out on the couch. All of a sudden things went haywire and woke me up from my nap. I saw my son Fredrick standing in the kitchen doorway, white as a sheet with a worried look on his little face. Behind Fredrick I seen my Husband's feet jerking very rapidly. I arose from the couch and went into the kitchen to check on Jim. My Husband was in a full grand mall seizure. As I neared him, I bent down to loosen his clothing at the same time telling Fredrick to get the bedspread and pillow from our bed. He did just that and helped me to cover his Daddy and put the pillow under Jim's head. I then put a spoon across his mouth so he could not bite his tongue. Yes I know, he could have broken his teeth but I did not have anything else that would have taken the pressure off his bite without hurting him. The spoon was better than nothing, he was lucky; he never bit his tongue or broke any teeth.

Once we had taken care of Jim, I phoned the Doctor and told him that my Husband was in a full grand mall seizure. The Doctor did not question me on it; he just took my word for it and asked what our Drug Store's phone number was. The Doctor had the Drug Store deliver Dilantin and Phenobarbital for epilepsy,

Jim had to be on this medication for the rest of his life. When he came out of that seizure, he felt like he tore every muscle in his body. It took a good week before the body stopped aching, he did not like what had happened and could not argue about what I had seen.

Because the dosage had to be worked out for his body weight and size, there were more than a few grand mall seizures. One of them took place at his work and needless to say, that grounded him in Winnipeg. He was no longer allowed to work on any moving objects or vehicles. He was what they called benched; he had to do his entire pipe fitting there. Others had to do the installation into the trains or boxcars. This was where he had to work for the rest of his workable days and he resented it right up to the end. It is very hard for a man to accept the diagnosis of epilepsy, as well as all the restrictions; it is a blow to their egos. In Jim's case, he did not know that anyone in his family had epilepsy, so did find it difficult to understand, why him? The next trip to Vancouver and a talk to his Mother gave him the answer. Apparently, in the translation of the Ukrainian language to English, seizures lost its meaning. There was an Uncle in the Ukraine that was really mean and did have seizures; he had drowned in his bath tub when he had one of them. This is one of the many reasons I find that has made me even more certain that epilepsy breaks down the mind; Jim is a good example of that.

This all had made Jim very angry as he did not believe he was an epileptic. He wanted to see and be tested by a specialist. The specialist put him into hospital and a barrage of tests were done. All of which proved that he was what he did not want to be, an epileptic. Come to think of it, he still did not believe it right up to his demise. This I could not figure out, why then did he keep having grand mall and mini seizures for the rest of his life? Just because he was not aware of what was occurring did not mean that they did not happen. His mental attitude changed slowly over the years; to me this was a reality. This was not make-believe as it was happening right in front of me. Maybe if he had accepted the reality, he would not have felt cheated. But then that is life, hard but true.

Very slowly and subtly, my Husband's personality began to change, though I really did not notice it at first. I do now, but that is because I am remembering how it was and what was happening. There would be signals to warn me of oncoming seizures, first there was the anger. This was followed by the accusations and just generally childish picky things, of course all aimed at me at first. When the onset of a mini-seizure would happen he would look straight at you, not see or acknowledge you, he just did not seem to be present at all. All of this would take approximately two minutes in time and sometimes even a little longer. Jim would let out a sigh and then start coming around to normal. He would never remember the missing space of time or have any personal indications as to what had taken place. He never had any "Halos" or any other kind of warning. He only knew what had happened after I told him.

In around this time period, Jim became involved in Professional Soccer. At first it was only at the team level, raising funds for them by having socials and card parties. He would have tickets printed up for draws on football and hockey games.

He started to help out running the different Youth Soccer Tournaments; it was at one of these that our boys and I really enjoyed ourselves. One Thanksgiving weekend, it was a Canadian Youth Tournament Championship with teams from all across Canada and all age groups. We were asked to help find places for some of the teams to billet down in. The teams we took were billeted at some of our friend's homes as well as at our Pastor's home. We ourselves billeted a full team in our home.

We did not find out until much later that two of the very young teams had no billet and were put up in a Motel. If I had known, they would have been taken care of by some more of our friends. The reason we did not hear about it until the weekend was almost over, they were not part of our responsibility. The boys would have had a better weekend. This I do know, as I found out, that I was pretty good at talking people into doing things they really did not want to do. I also found that I enjoyed the challenge of the whole thing, it raised my adrenalin. What a weekend it was for us though, it was fully packed with fun and excitement. The team that stayed with us had a real ball, never a dull moment here.

In our house, our sons all slept in sleeping bags on the kitchen floor; they gladly gave up their rooms to the soccer players. When the boys started arriving, they found out that our four year old could read with no trouble at all. Fredrick was self taught off the bus and truck advertisements, he also belonged to the Library at that time. On one of the bags there was a tag that said: "Rick the Prick." When the young man heard Fredrick read it out loud, all the name tags were removed immediately. Of course, Fredrick just thought it was great to be able to read it, so did I. The choice of words were just was not my bag, but that was okay too. It was quite awhile before he learned what the words really meant, he did find out eventually.

Let me say that it really did get hectic at times, reason being, I cooked three big meals that weekend. One day it was ham, another it was roast beef and on the final day it was turkey with the stuffing. The team really enjoyed their meals; they all ate heartily and even did a little sightseeing. They ate only two meals a day, a very light breakfast and a really good meal at supper time. I even had a chance to see some of the games, the semi-finals and the final. Because making a turkey dinner took very little attention thus giving me some time to go and watch a game. Besides, the park where they played their games was only a block and a half away from our home.

When it was all over, I sent them all home with

turkey, ham and roast beef sandwiches, cookies, cake, fresh fruit and pop. For those who were allowed to drink, they received a bottle of beer. The boys that had to stay in a motel room, I also made up sandwiches for them and gave them the treats and chocolate milk to drink. They were all very young players and what I did for them was greatly appreciated. I know this as they sent me a special thank you card after they returned home. Through all the years, we kept in touch with them all and in some cases, still do.

As our boys grew up, there were times that Jim's temper was extreme; it was at those times that their friends had to stay away. Other times, it was an open door policy for all of their friends. They were welcome and treated like family members; we did enjoy it a lot. When it could be no more, it was missed very much; those were wonderful times in my life.

We would play chess, checkers, sometimes even cribbage or rummy. It was when the games started losing their rules and had become Jim's rules. No amount of showing him the written rules or reading them to him would change his mind. It was his way or else, well we all chose the or else, no games at all, it just was not worth the hassle with Jim.

Oh yes, all of the boys' friends did know what was wrong with Jim, we never hide it; at least they were able to understand why they could not come in some of the time. Those were the years that all our sons were in a Boys Group, also were into baseball, football, soccer and hockey. Our youngest Fredrick, just loved to play table tennis and catch with me, he never gave up on the games we played together. We were part of the Parents participation in the Boys Group. This was the only thing that Jim took part in with the boys; because of one bad apple in the organization, he quit that also. Me, I stayed with it as long as I was allowed to, I just loved planning their special breakfasts and dinner banquets. I became adept at talking to food processing companies and grocery stores into donating meats as well as other food items. They did not mind donating anything as it was Church affiliated and a non-profit organization. Actually, there were times when there was too much given and there was a lot left over. They would sell what was left to the attending parents thus raising a little extra money to do something else with.

In sports, I was the one who attended most of their games, sometimes by Cab when there was no bus available to the area. There were also times that coaches had to work and could not come to the game. Those were the times that the boys would elect me temporary coach. When that happened, I would buy them a treat after their game whether they won or not. It was a hot chocolate in winter and ice cream in the summer, the trouble was, it did not happen often enough.

At this period of time in my life, I was allowed to

go to Church and Worship. I was still in the choir; that was really great for me, though I do not know if I was ever a good singer. To me it was so enjoyable and gave me an outing at Christmas and Easter time, a break to be by myself. I love GOD and I know He has been with me all through the years; He has forgiven me for all of my sins. He is with me now and always will be, He has truly touched me and is my driving force.

During this time, Ted had made many friends in his school. There was only one that is worth mentioning. He turned out to be his very best friend of all. This young mans' name is Jack; he was a tall drink of water and a constant joker and visitor. Jack never expected anything of anyone and always made sure life was a joy at all times. When here visiting, he quite often played games with Ted and me. He never hesitated to give a helping hand, especially when I was doing dishes. The only problem was, he just could not resist fooling around. One day he had me at the sink with only a days worth of dishes laughing for two and half hours. I was getting to a point of frustration with his joking so I crowned him with a pot. He said: "Ow that hurt" and we all laughed after that. To my knowledge he still carries that mark across the bridge of his nose from the pot. I still am friends with his Mother and see her often at bowling. Along with his sisters and brothers, the friendship has spanned many years, no regrets what ever. Ted did not want a funeral only a cremation; this did hurt Jack a lot. Jack I am sorry but I had to respect

Ted's wishes. I pray you will understand and wish you the best in your life. You are such a happy person and have such a good soul.

When Jim was involved with the Professional Soccer movement, he took care of the then Alexander Park along with all it buildings and stands. He became Referee in Chief and a board member. It was during this time that I decided to help him out and become his secretary. At least this way I helped out and did not feel useless. He still would not let me go back to school to become a certified public accountant, there were many arguments over that. I was told many times that I was not smart enough to do it, so why waste the money? He never did say that in a nice way, he was belligerent every time with the additional not so nice words and phrases. I know, should have said something back, sometimes I did but it did absolutely no good, I was told not to spout off my rights to him. You know that never once did I ever mention my rights to him, guess the words that I did use made him think that was my meaning.

Still and all, the boys did help out at the park. They learned how to put in sod, ride the mower to cut the grass and mark the field before each game. They also helped me to clean up the dressing rooms along with the washrooms and boardroom. There were a lot of gopher holes on the field; we had to fill them and set out bait to destroy those rodents. If we did not, the players could and often did get injured on the field. We had a dog at that time, it was a Basenji; he was absolutely gopher crazy. He often would dig and make the holes even larger, he loved to chase the rodents and cause general mischief. The dogs' name was Zotz, he could not bark and was often troublesome, but our youngest Fredrick just loved him to bits. When we set out bait, we had to stop bringing the dog to the park. We later found that we had a wild resident weasel in the park, it was then we ceased putting out the bait. It was the only solution to keep the weasel alive and let him do the job he was meant to do. Assuming that it was a he, it was a truly beautiful animal with such a lovely coat of fur, not only that, he did his job really well. He not only caught a lot of gophers but he also rid us of mice, it was nice to have the buildings free of them.

Everyday I would take our two dogs for a walk but not together, Zotz was too aggressive and would fight with the other one. When I had Sparky with me on one of our walks, I had a very brief vision of our street of many years before. It had a gravel road and only one house, for that moment in time, my dog was no longer with me. In a blink of an eye, everything was back to normal. This had startled me and left me feeling a little frightened too. I have not had another vision like it, do not know why or what it means, once was enough for me.

One year, I was given the opportunity to run the Canteen, (concession stand) at Alexander Park. With being the Secretary of the Board it was a very active time for me. It was also relatively free of the bad mouth from my Husband; he was too busy to be petty and argumentative; he had enough from others at the park. I redecorated the canteen, did a pretty good job of running it, the reason I know this is the teams always complimented me on it. If I had of done poorly, they would never have ordered anything from me again.

What they liked the most was that they could pre-order their hot dogs, hamburgers, fries, hot chocolate and coffee. After the game everything was hot and ready for them to enjoy. Personally, I did not ever take to fast foods, it did not matter if I made it or not. When I did make fries it was with very fresh oil in my deep fryer, I really believe that is what they liked, nothing was ever greasy.

My son Fred and his friend John always helped me there. Took care to pay them fairly on the jobs that they did; they were very good workers. If Jim had his way, they would have been working for nothing; I do not see it that way. Children do not learn properly when working for nothing, plus it just is not fair to them. I do not regret any hard work we had to do; it was an exciting time in our lives. At that time, there was a little girl and her bother that I cared for during the week; they also worked with me in the canteen during tournaments on the weekends. The girl was cute and often received more sales and tips because of her looks, it made her brother angry. Those two would go into the stands, get order and then take the orders back when ready for their customers. Doing it this way prevented long line-ups in front of the Canteen and made it easier to serve everyone faster. These two children worked real hard and earned every penny they received, not to mention that they loved doing it. That Christmas, they were able to purchase gifts for their Parents without asking for extra money. I paid all my workers by the work that they did, never did short change anyone; guess that is why they liked to work for me. On the other hand, if one just sat around doing nothing but talk, that was what they received, nothing.

One day Jim received a phone call from his Sister. I told him while he was listening on the phone to her that one of our nieces had tried to take her own life. He was amazed that I was saying the same thing as his Sister was. I was just saying it in a matter of fact way as if it was no surprise to me at all; it was very scary to me. Receiving these kinds of vibes by the phone was truly unbelievable. I am very close to our nieces and that is why I receive these ominous signals, it does scare me a lot. Usually I just get that scared feeling in my tummy when something happens. When this happens I try and get in touch with others to find out what is happening. Most times, I receive a call from the family before I can track down the problem.

A few months later, a second call from Jim's

Sister, once again I knew she was on the phone and what she was saying to him about our other niece, her daughter. As he was listening to both of us he was hearing word for word the exact same thing. Our niece had a ruptured appendix and was in hospital with peritonitis, she was seriously ill. This again shocked Jim as I should not have received those vibes. As I said before, it was because of the closeness to my nieces. That niece was in hospital for months before she was clear of all infection. Even then she was watched very closely as she became very susceptible to any new infection. Both of these nieces are okay and very much alive. They are now Grandmothers.

All during the time that Jim was at Alexander Park, he would have unpredictable times with a very bad temper. He would bad mouth not only me and the boys but at times even the players or members of the board. Mostly it was the boys and I, it was not nice to hear or see. Sometimes when someone came to our rescue he even bad mouthed them, of course we knew what was going to occur; the other people did not. Mostly this kind of action by my Husband took place behind our doors and no one ever heard what was going on. Within a couple of days he would have a mini-seizure. After that he would not remember what took place at all, it was completely lost to him. As you well know, this did not make it any less painful, it was also never forgotten. We just went on with our lives, what else could one do?

After a few years of working at Alexander Park, our youngest Fredrick was into his teenage years. He started having a life of his own, along with that, he had to make many new decisions on what road he was going to take.

It was about that time that another group became interested in the running of the canteen at the park. They received permission and it was all done without consulting me about it. The courtesy of asking me if I still wanted to run it; just was not there, to me that was unfair. Those men of the "Old School" had no manners; I would never do this to anyone. To top it, they wanted me to leave all the items that I had paid for. That I would have done if they paid me for them, but no, that is not what they wanted, they wanted to get them for nothing. No way, I took everything home that was mine, the old refrigerator and old deep fryer was left for them to re-hook up. By the way, they were clean and ready for use, no odours or anything. While I ran the canteen, I had stored those items and kept them covered. The rest of the canteen was in great shape, it was bright and clean. All the counters had quality covering not that cheap plastic that was there before.

It was about this time that our son Ted decided to join the Armed Forces. This lasted approximately a year and a half; he just could not take or follow orders. He eventually received a Dishonourable discharge for insubordination. That was all before his term was up of course. You see, they still did not find out what was wrong with him either. Everything that had happened was everybody else's fault, never Ted's; he could not accept the responsibility of his own shortcomings.

When Ted came home, he decided to return to school. At first he wanted to become a mason, (brick layer), than decided that he did not like it and quit. A little later he once again decided to return to school and become an Engineer. This time he loved the course and often asked his Dad to help him over the rough spots. It was the first time that Jim and Ted had something in common and did not argue about anything. They sat many times together and worked out a lot of the problems. At this time, I thought that just maybe Jim could have become an Engineer; he seemed to understand it a lot. He said no, that he was too old to do that now, of course I differ with that, but there was no point in discussing it. It just was not going to be, I often wondered if he was just afraid to try or maybe it was because of his epilepsy, who knows?

Ted found his first Engineering job with one of the Medical Groups, there was a problem there but we never did find out what. With Ted, if he did not want you to know, he would never tell you. After that Ted applied for work at one of the large hospitals, he was hired and once again that did not last long. The person who was his boss, so Ted said, was really obnoxious and a very strict disciplinarian. He was just like Ted and of course, he just could not take it and quit that job as well. Two people with the same personality will eventually clash, that was probably what happened that time. The next job he was hired to do was at a hockey arena, that one worked out real well and lasted quite a few years.

Chapter Nine

It was during this time that Ted had met and fell in love with a beautiful young lady named Lorraine. I just loved her immediately and still do; I do not think she knows that though, well maybe. She was a very self centered person and very difficult to get close too, just maybe, she was afraid to have a relationship with me. Jim did not like her from the very start, he refused to go to their social or wedding, he would not give an inch on this matter. Thinking back on it, maybe he knew that he could not control her at all, her personality was too strong. Then again, maybe I am giving him too much credit on knowing when he would lose in a relationship. He was very angry with me when I had decided that I would make Lorraine's wedding dress. I did it anyway; I was not going to let him spoil this day for me or anyone else.

I love to create things for people according to their size, looks and what suited their personalities. This is one skill that I still have, I see the person in that item I am about to make for them before even getting started. To me, all of Lorraine's petite features made her suitable for a Southern Belle style of gown, which is how she looked in my mind. That was exactly the style of dress I made for her, she was simply beautiful in her wedding gown. It was her personality, fit to a "T".

With her wedding gown, Lorraine wore a white

wide brimmed hat with a white satin bow and trailing ribbons. Her bouquet had baby's breath, white carnations, yellow roses and a single purple orchid in the centre. It also had trailing white ribbons with a yellow rose bud on each end. Her attendants wore very nicely fitted yellow dresses with white wide brimmed hats minus the trailing ribbons. They carried nosegays of white and yellow carnations with trailing yellow ribbons. The Ushers and the Groom wore western styled tuxedos of beige and brown with yellow carnation boutonnieres, it was truly a beautiful wedding.

All during this time, I was also making costumes for the dancers and baton twirlers at the community centre. What an experience that was. I became so good at it that there was very little wastage of fabric. I bought the fabric in large amounts, pinned and cut them all out as the costumes were needed. This way the cost to the Parents was greatly reduced, it cost enough for the trims, which was the real expensive part of their costumes. I did this for quite a few years, much to the disappointment of my Husband.

With the left over fabric I would make doll clothes at Christmas time and the community centre would sell them at their bazaar. When I gave them to the community centre, the volunteers would purchase them without the dolls clothes ever reaching the tables. I do know that they liked it when I did this for them as they were never duplicated by anyone else. Whenever I do find the time, I still love to make these things for the community centre; it is a real challenge to make things children do love.

Even then my Husband complained like crazy but really could not stop me from doing this; it was all a part of me that enjoyed making pretty things. He was not in poor health then and did not need my full attention as yet. He did resent it though, the thing is, I kept up with all of my work and still made costumes and doll clothes during the day. He was at work and the boys were in school, so he had no leg to stand on when it came to what I was doing, it cost him nothing. That did not stop the bad mouth from him, it was always there and it made me very miserable.

I did have one other problem; the Mothers of the children did not like to do the sewing of the trims on their costumes. This I did not understand, they all knew how to sew, could they not sew the trims on their children's costumes? Too much was expected of me, so I ended up charging them $5.00 per costume that I worked on, this covered any out of pocket expense. I did this to stop the demands on my time, money out of their pockets they did not want. When it did become too much for me, I had to quit. It was a real heart breaker for the children; they knew that they no longer could depend on me. I was my own worst enemy, did not know how to say no. I did learn how to say it but still have a problem with it, it all depends on how and what I am asked to do. Sometimes it also depends on who asks me to do something for them.

Not long after Ted and Lorraine were married, Ted changed jobs again, this time it was for an Insurance company. Lorraine also went back to work for a well known grocery firm. It was sometime later that Lorraine was diagnosed with Hypoglycaemia; she had to eat less but more often during the day. If she did not do so she would go into uncontrollable rages for no good reason, this made their marriage a living hell. Lorraine did not want to eat the way she was instructed to. It was like being on the outside looking in whenever she went into one of her rages. Between Ted's constant accusations, suspicions and her uncontrollable temper, their marriage broke up. I was and still am truly glad that this union produced no children as both of their health problems would have been handed down. Also believe that they would have been very poor parents, they were too involved with themselves in other words; they were very selfish.

I cannot remember how many times that Jim told me that I was just plain ignorant and stupid. I chose to ignore it and stored it in the back of my mind. There was just too much going on in my life to keep letting Jim get to me, it was not worth the hassle. As for the housework, how does one clean the house around his pack-rat collections? This consisted of newspapers, fliers, empty envelopes, empty Kleenex boxes and Lord knows what else. It just grew larger over the years, I was never allowed to touch any of it, if I dared to, I was yelled at, it was just not worth it. Besides the pack-rat items there was the uncompleted projects. There was very little room to move through the house, one cannot clean under these circumstances.

It was during all this stress that Ted tried to take his life many times. He drove his car into a telephone pole as well as buildings, each time there were bruises and but no serious injuries, he survived every incident. These actions sent him to a Psychiatrist and he was finally diagnosed as a manic-depressive. That was when I realized what had made Ted out of sorts all of his life. We were never able to figure it out, sure was glad at last there was a name for it. Of course, when you have never met a person under the same condition, how do you recognize it? We were not psychiatrists, so we should not have expected so much of ourselves, but that is exactly what parents do. We did not blame others but Ted did, we did not make him that way.

Come to think of it, he had an aunt on his Father's side that was much like him and did eventually pass away in a car accident. Her boy friend at that time was also a manic-depressive and drove the car into a telephone pole, he survived, and she did not. She had left her baby behind; I wonder if the problem carried on, it must have, someone else was left with the problem to care for. That could and would be a true heartbreak for them.

Jim never did understand or accept the diagnosis and he refused to believe that Ted had a problem. The Insurance Company that Ted worked for placed him on disabililty as he was uncontrollable at times. When one loses control at work, the company has no choice but to place you on disability, there are no room for errors. It is dangerous to keep that person on the job especially in Engineering. Ted ended up in the psychiatric ward many times to get regulated. There were times he was not even allowed to go out for a cup of coffee or a package of cigarettes. At those times, I would go to see Ted and bring him both, also tried to bring a little cheer. Sometimes that worked but most times it did not, the depression stood in the way, I tried anyway with the hope of succeeding. In my heart and mind I do not believe that they have found a way to control manic-depressive people. If they have, I do not know of anyone that it has worked on; sincerely hope there is a way, as it must be pure hell to be the patient.

When Ted was out of the psychiatric ward, I spent many a night talking to him on the phone so he would not try to take his life. I often told him how precious life was and that it was the only life he was going to have, please accept and take care of it. Also during this time, between the situation with Ted and Jim's mouth; I was having a really bad time of it, I did pay the price for it. Sometimes no matter how hard you try to ignore hurtful things and try to be bright, it bothers you anyway, it sure did me.

Chapter Ten

It all came to a head for me on November 16th. 1981; this was when I was having severe chest pains. I could not talk and had great difficulty breathing at this time; it was hard for me to attract my Husbands attention. My body was in a complete cold sweat. It happened many times earlier but with no pain. I went slowly to Jim and rattled the newspaper he was reading and holding my burning arms trying to show him that I was really ill. When he finally realized that I was in great distress, he called our Doctor and was told to take me to the hospital immediately. The logic of a woman took over, one cannot go to hospital all sweaty, and a bath you must have. I was in a cold sweat for a few days actually, could smell myself, did not want anyone to say that I was not clean, go figure. I could have died at that time; I surely did tempt God's patience that day. I am forever grateful to Him for allowing me to stay alive, without Him, I would not have survived. He must still have more for me to complete in this lifetime or He would not have kept me here.

My youngest son Fredrick drove me to hospital in his truck for some much needed assistance. They took one look at me and rushed me straight into the examining rooms. They took some of my blood for testing, also x-rays and an EKG. All during this time, Fredrick wanted to see me right away, he was truly worried. They would not let him in, they told him that I was naked; he did not want to see me that way did he? Of course he did as he only wanted to see that I was okay. I believe that in Fredrick's state of mind he would not have noticed me being naked; this would never have been a problem for him.

They decided that I had a heart attack and that the reason for it was my potassium level. It was way too low and it almost killed me. In my IV there was heart, blood pressure and potassium medications all going through, it burned like crazy. The ambulance was called to transfer me to another hospital once I was stabilized. Apparently it was one very busy time for sick people; they just did not have a bed for me in their ICU (Intensive Care Unit). While I was being transported by ambulance to the other hospital, my son Fredrick was following us all the way. When settled in, they allowed Fredrick to visit me, once he seen that I was in good hands, he returned home.

Let me say, you never want potassium going through an IV into your veins; it burns and causes much swelling and pain in your arm. Sometimes the arm becomes so inflamed and no pain killer helps, the only thing that gives any relief is alternating hot and cold pads. They put me on oxygen because I had low readings and that helped to keep me in the ICU for twelve days. It took that long to get my heart back to a normal beat; my heartbeat was a gallop like a horses trot, really strange. One nurse let me listen to her heart, then my heart, the difference was really outstanding. In the ICU, there was not a radio or television as that is where the really ill people are placed. To top it, I was not allowed to do puzzle books, read a newspaper or a book. The reason for that was you have to keep your arms down in order for the IV to work properly and not become plugged.

For a person who was so much on the go all the time and all of a sudden nothing to do, it was a very rude awakening as to how fragile a person is, life is ever so precious. After the twelve days of trying to get me regulated, they shipped me upstairs to a ward; that was where I spent the next ten days. I thought I was feeling pretty good, much to my surprise I found out that only my ego told me I was okay. When I tried to pick up a little girl the pain from lifting her was excruciating. I had better behave myself, slow down and take good care of myself.

It was then that the Doctors told me that second hand smoke and stress was the reason that this had happened to me. I thought that it was the low potassium that was the culprit; they said that was another reason too. At that time, I did not realize that what they were saying was true. Now I do believe it and fully understand how close I came to dying, I was one of the lucky ones. The Doctors gave me only five more years to live, I had decided then that I was going to make the best of those years. I learned to cook and eat healthy; a lot of raw fruit and vegetables, little or no fried foods at all would be the best bet for a healthy life. I have done pretty good over the time, still have to watch because it is so easy to fall back on your diet and not resist temptation. Considering the stress on top of it, I would say that it is a miracle for me to be still alive, GOD has a lot to do with that, don't you think?

Exercise is also a part of the component, walking is the best bet and that I do a lot of. My Doctor of today says walk, walk some more and even walk more on top of that, it is what I do. Well everyone, all of my Doctors who gave me only an additional five years of life are now deceased. It only goes to show you that they may think they know you but in fact they are only guessing. You have to make up your own mind on what is right and not play games with yourself, if you do not follow this, you will not survive. Just remember this, it also depends on your will power and our Lord's help, I do know this with all of my heart.

You must push away from the table before you are finished, do not snack unless it is raw fruit or vegetables and then to walking. Whatever you do, stay away from the weighing machine, it will be your down fall. When you start taking good care of yourself, that is what you are doing, replacing fat with muscle, muscle is heavier than fat. You can see what I am getting at, can't you? When I had my heart attack, I was only forty-eight years old; I am now seventy-two. I also never had an operation on my heart, not even an angioplasty done. My survival was a combined effort by me and my Lord, without Him I would not be here.

When I left the hospital, I took everything very slowly, and as I improved I began to return to normal. By that I mean, being able to do more and above all gain my strength back. That in it self took a long time, so those who read this, remember it does not happen overnight. At that time I decided to join a SPA, which I truly believe helped me out a lot, it made me get strong faster. Of course Jim did not believe this at that time, I am still here, he is not. Also I believe that my job here on earth is not complete, that is why I am here, God Has Blessed Me! Even at that, I must do my part the best way I can, continue to eat right and exercise as much as my body will let me. Also one must get away from the stress that drives ones life, it can destroy you. These are all the components that are important in staying alive. Pay attention to all the warnings your body gives you, do not ignore anything. Do not say to yourself that the warning you have received, is just something usual. Do not go on with what you are doing as it just might kill you. If you get a pain or a heavy pressure in your chest or between your shoulder blades, head for the nearest hospital emergency room, do no wait.

I have to tell you about some of my son Fredrick's friends, they are a good group of boys and now are young men. They were a part of our lives that must not be forgotten even though some things were not very pleasant, all the more reason to remember them by.

First there is a young man named Bruce, nicknamed Jinxy. That was because he was never lucky at guessing the winners on the football, basketball, hockey and baseball teams. He could never win on a wager as he was wrong most of the time, rarely guessed the right outcome. This young man was born with "cerebral palsy" and his body was twisted in many different ways. He went through many operations in order to become mobile. At first he was a brat, but then who isn't at some time in their lives? As he grew up, he did mellow out. He lost his Father to a heart attack when he was very young. It took a long time before he realized it was not anybody's fault that this did happen. His Father was a soccer player and was just not as lucky as I was. It may have been a different type of heart attack.

Jinxy became a part of our lives and spent much time with us; we had a lot of fun together. When over here, we played chess, card games and listened to a lot of music, we just loved the same music as he did. When Fredrick and Jinxy were left to their ways, they did manage to get into trouble together. One time they even caused a fire in the house. That was when I smelled the smoke and went into Fredrick's room. The mattress had caught fire from some foolish experiment,

Jinxy had his head stuck out the window gasping for air. I managed to put out the fire and believe it or not, Fredrick was still able to sleep on his bed. All the stuffing I pulled out of the mattress was replaced with old towels and anything else I could find. Until we could afford to purchase a new mattress, this one had to last and it did okay for awhile.

Well that is not all. Jinxy trained hard to become a Lab. Tech., one who draws blood from patients, and then he would go to the laboratory. He would work up what tests he had to do on the blood and urine for the medical staff. He did real well at this and would still be doing so until now except for one reason. He found a job in Saskatchewan in one of the hospitals and was really enjoying the work there. The problem was; that he missed going to his Church on Sundays. That was when another religious group came into the picture. In my opinion, they conned him into believing that only their religion could cure his twisted body. Of course we know that would never happen and it has not happened but he still believes; only God can give this Miracle. They made a liar, cheat and a sneak out of that precious young man; it also made me very angry as I love him like a son. I had to tell him to leave his new religion outside of my house as I could not tolerate it. If he left it behind, he was still welcome anytime. He would not leave the religion outside the door. I sincerely hope he is okay and I shall never forget him; we had a lot of great times together. May GOD Bless Him Always!

Now for the young man named Albert. Fredrick and Albert were together from grade one, they used to tell each other jokes, which we often overheard, they were just great. They did get into mischief a few times together; I promised not to tell what or how, as it would be very embarrassing to both of them now. Another time though, they could not resist the temptation of taking money from Albert's Dad's wallet, boy did that cause a commotion. There was a lot of yelling, not that it did any good, but it did stop them from helping themselves to what was not theirs. We loved that time in our lives, even the short comings we cannot forget, it is all part of one's being.

One Halloween, Fredrick dressed up as a devil; he wore red horns, red turtle neck sweater, red tights and carried a home made pitchfork coloured in with red crayon. Albert dressed in his Dad's old shirt, tie, patched pants that was rolled up and an old black hat and jacket. Daniel was in a blue turtle neck sweater, a tutu made out of sheer curtain fabric in layers and it stood out beautifully. He also wore a pair of white tights and had make-up on his face, it was just great, no one recognized Daniel at all. That was a Halloween to remember, the only problem was it snowed that night and they came home looking like snowmen. What a sight it was, worth every effort.

There was another young man named John, he was truly a lost soul. His Father was an alcoholic and abused him terribly. When he found us, he was in our hearts to stay, just like a son that should have been. He would walk in the door and go to the coffee pot; he would not only enjoy his friendship with Fredrick but also with Jim and me. If there was no coffee made, he knew where everything was, how to make it and would go ahead and do so. One day he came over and found that our coffee machine was broken; that was when he had to have instant coffee but not for long.

That Christmas, John gave me a gift, of course wouldn't you know it; it was a coffee maker. That gift to me was more for himself I know but the thought was there. It was just great, it did not matter to me that it was needed and used by all of us. We treated John like a son which made Fredrick ever so happy, he was so much a part of us, love for him was there and without question.

When I had my heart attack, it was on John's Birthday; he came to the hospital to see me, all worried but relieved to see that I was okay. All these friends of my sons came to see me there including the girls. When I was asked if the were family, no hesitation whatever, yes they are all my family. My husband Jim was the only one who never came to see me, not even once, he could have at anytime. In the ICU there is no visiting hours when it comes to family, only three at one time are allowed to come in to see you.

John's Mother went to Germany to see her family members she had not seen for a very long time. She asked if John could stay with us, of course the answer was yes. While he was here, there was a graduation he was involved in, we had the opportunity to decorate his car and take pictures of it and him. We never made so many pom-poms in our lives; it was just super and a lot of fun. I bought the pom-pom kits and we made John's car look extra special, he really liked that. He also worked with us at one time at Alexander Park and truly enjoyed it. John worked hard just like our boys did, Jinxy did whenever he received the opportunity. These were truly wonderful times in our lives; I know they all would agree with me on this. It is a part of my life and that is why it is now in my book.

Chapter Eleven

Come June 1982, my Husband, son Fredrick and John, planned to go to a fishing derby together. It was a Friday afternoon when Jim came home with severe chest pain. I gave him one of my nitro-glycerine tablets but it only helped for a little while. He needed to take another tablet because the pain returned. I phoned Fredrick and he came over to take his Dad to hospital, in that time period, I had to give Jim three more tablets. When Fredrick arrived, we all got into his vehicle and went to the hospital.

At the door, Jim handed his package of cigarettes over to Fred and told him to keep them. He just had his last cigarette and would never need them again. Jim was right, he did it cold turkey; he never puffed on another cigarette. The only trouble was, it was already too late; that is on hindsight of course. Jim did have a severe heart attack, worse than what I had, morphine was the only pain medication that quieted his pain down. When they x-rayed him, they found old scar tissue; it was at least ten years old so they said. That scar tissue indicated that this was not his first heart attack. He did have one previously and was lucky to be alive.

Apparently he would have had chest pain or a heavy pressure to indicate that he was in dire straights. He probably ignored it; we are our own worst enemies, we often never learn from our experiences or warnings, I sure can believe that. Well at least Fred and John were able to go on that fishing derby. Jim of course never made it and to my knowledge never went on any other fishing derby either. He did go to Lockport with Ted a few times to fish and I do believe that he went at least once more with Fred and John. That was a regular fishing trip and because of Jim's health, this activity was severely curtailed.

Jim had to go on disability and it was not until December 1982 that the Doctor gave the go ahead to return to work. He was only forty-seven years old at that time and the railroad told him that he must retire. By doing this, Jim missed out on what they called the Golden Handshake, ($45,000.00) by three and a half years. To top it, to receive a full pension, he had to pay for the pension deductions that would have been taken off his pay if he had of worked. We had to borrow the money to cover that added expense and also to cover the time that we would not receive a pension cheque. For the deductions, we borrowed from our credit union. For the time that we did not receive a pension cheque we borrowed from our son Fred, thank goodness for loved ones. When the first pension cheque came in, it had all the arrears on it so we were able to clear up all our debt; that was including to our son Fred. The railroad pension was a disability one which included a small stipend from the OAS (old age security). This was Jim's choice as he did not think he would last long enough to get the full OAS. He also received disability from the other pension plan; we were okay for awhile until he turned sixty years of age. When he did, the railroad pension reverted to the regular pension amount minus the stipend, which was a monthly loss of about $500.00. The other pension also reverted to the normal amount too, that was cut by half of the disability amount. The real problem was that it caused a severe drop in our monthly income. It was tough going for about four years, which would be when I would receive my OAS. I did apply for the supplement but never receive it as even with all the loss it still was too much income.

The irony was it should not have been that rough on us, it was just that Jim spent so much on Lottery tickets. I really believe that it would not have been as hard on us if Jim had stopped his gambling. Anyway he was one angry person; he thought he was taken for a ride. Of course he thought that, but it was the rules of his company and he knew it, everyone else had to live by those rules too, Jim was no exception. He never had the golden handshake in the first place so why be so angry? If he had of received it and then it was taken away, then I could see being angry, his anger was totally self destructive. Jim would not even go to his own retirement party; he was only spiting himself in doing that. He gave me many days of mouth and arguments over this golden handshake. This kind of anger only belongs in the garbage as nothing could ever be done about it. If he had of received this golden handshake, I do believe he would have blown it all on Lottery tickets.

One day I told him that I wanted this anger gone by the time I returned from the SPA, he did just that but only for a little while. His brother Peter phoned him while I was at the SPA; he lied to Jim by telling him that I was fooling around on him, not with just one guy, but with many. Of course this just was not true, I would not do that to him but he chose to believe his brother. At my SPA there were no men only women as I attended it on ladies days only. There was nothing that I could say or do to get him to believe me, he just believed his brother. Do you know what? He believed what his brother told him right up to his passing, what a misery he made for himself. One of the reasons he did not believe me, that is, what I think is the reason, the medications he was on made him impotent. When I was told this by his Doctors, I had decided right then that I would not worry about the sexual part of our marriage. I would simply shut myself down; this was something that Jim did not believe any woman could do. Please believe me when I say, if one puts their mind to do something, no matter what it is, they can and will succeed. I am not the only one who has been able to do so, all it takes is a strong will; for me another man is totally out of the question. Two bad marriages are enough in one life time and I do know others who agree with me on that. I fill my life with many things and they keep me not only busy but extremely happy and young in feeling, yes it is possible.

One day I came home from the SPA and found Jim stripping the walls in the front bedroom, it was because water had seeped in between the walls. Everything had moulded right through to the siding. Jim showed me the wood and plasterboard that had the mould; there was quite a lot in two areas. Even the part that had none had to be torn away to be sure it was all cleaned out. The real problem was that he had taken on too big of a job. His health problems flared up again so he did not complete the work, he never improved after that. The room was never finished; am hoping that Daniel and I will be able to complete the job one day. Until then, or if I hire someone to do it for me at a reasonable rate, it will remain unfinished. As for the insulation, plastic sheeting and wallboard, it is all here in the attic or behind my couch. The only thing that has to be purchased is the paint and the carpet.

Over the years that same room became Jim's catch all for his pack-rat items. He had moved all of it into the front room when he started to work on it. There were old newspapers, fliers and magazines to name a few; they were all packed into boxes and garbage bags. When he found he could not continue; once again it was stacked in that front bedroom.

The only good thing about it was that I was actually able to get around my front room to vacuum and dust, I was not able to do that for a long time. Of course, that did not last too long as Jim found more things to save and stack in the front room. He put boxes after boxes under the dining room table and even purchased two metal cabinets to use. Every bit of space in our own bedroom was stuffed full of junk, especially the closet; we could not hang anything that was coat length in there. All the items that had been placed on the floor of the closet made very little room for one's clothing. Our room is small in the first place, he had managed to make it even smaller, and of course I had no say in the matter as usual.

It was around about this time that Jim had received a call from his sister; he answered the phone and I once again knew what she was saying to him. His sister told him that she had had a severe heart attack and was now confined to her home as she was on oxygen. His sister also had trouble breathing because of her smoking all of those years, just like Jim. Knowing what was being said without hearing really made my Husband upset. The reason was he just could not understand how this could happen to me. It was just at that time, I was very close to his sister so received her vibes when they were on the telephone with each other. Though Jim did not know it, these incidents did scare and upset me also, it was almost like mind reading and leaving no privacy for them. I did not know what was said on anything else they talked about, just about the illness. I must say that this happens only because I am close to the person who is ill, and it is always on the phone. Any other feelings I get has to be tracked down,

I usually hear from them or another member of the family first.

To continue on with the story of our lives, Jim had developed a blockage in his bowel area. They thought at first it was a knot that was causing him the problems. He was in severe pain; could not hold his food down and was throwing up bile, what a mess. He was admitted to hospital to get the area pumped out once again it took about a week. This had happened many times over the years and it really made him very miserable and unhappy. He also developed a hernia in the groin, operation number one.

Chapter Twelve

Sometime during this time period, our youngest son Fred had met his future Wife. Her name is Tina Marie, what a lovely person she is and the daughter that we never did have, we love her dearly. They are a perfect match, could not have asked for better. After a while, the two of them moved in with us, and over time, there were many, many arguments by Jim. This action eventually forced them to move out on their own in a very peaceful and lovely little place. A while later, Fred had to move once again as his job required him to be closer to his work, eventually Jim made amends with Fred. I am telling you that Jim was very hard on Fred and generally made him miserable when they were together. It was like an irresistible urge on Jims part, it was just plain mean and unfair. Fred never deserved anything like this; maybe it is because Jim realized that Fred and I were so close and best friends, jealousy maybe? The problem was that Jim rarely remembered doing this to Fred, this never made it any easier on him, Fred I mean. When he reads this, Fred will know how much I love him and really do care, that will never change and he _is_ my best friend, he always will be.

Of course during all those trying times, I took so much bad mouth from Jim, some I understand was from being ill but still, that is no excuse for what he did. There were accusations of me fooling around but also that I was spending money on nonsense. Let me say, I could stop this and did over time, how? Well, I set up a bookkeeping system; it was very simple and easy to read and understand. Believe it or not, it did save me many, many arguments. I had pages for every-thing that both Jim and I had spent. I made entries every day that money was used to purchase something. Nothing was too small to enter, it had to be that way or it would not have worked. Jim was too picky so it all had to be very accurate and to top it; all of the sales slips had to be kept. If I did not do it this way, I would not be able to prove anything, it was just that terrible.

There was a special section called "Lotteries." Every amount on what ticket by name that was bought, this was noted in this section. When there were winners this section also was where I entered it, on what and how much of course. I hated these scratch tickets with all my heart; I did without too much over them. After setting this up and making all of the entries on everything spent in such detail; there were still some accusations made. At that time, I would get the books and put them in his lap; I would then tell him to look for himself. If he did not, I would then turn to each section and show him the totals and on what. The lotteries were usually the highest amounts. He often would send the books flying in anger, after a while, he never threw them again. Later that same day he would say to me: "Did I really spend that much on lotteries?" Of course he did and I proved it; not only by the books and all the entries but by the receipts as well as the tickets. When he still doubted me on this, I would produce the tickets, often they were dated. The ones that were not dated he knew, they were the ones he kept track of by the code numbers at the bottom of each ticket. I would total everything up in a neat file and show him, he would then see that I was right every time. I had to be or my neck would be in a sling again, would not dare to try and fool Jim, it just would not be worth the risk.

Later that same year, Fred and Tina came over for a visit, reason; she showed us he engagement ring. They told us that they set their Wedding Date for July 18th. 1988. What a wonderful surprise that was, you do not know how happy that made us. Maybe you have gone through the same or similar thing and do know how happy we were. They had already made expensive wedding plans and thus would not be able to go on a honeymoon. After a long talk together, it was decided that they would go a little less expensive. I do not know if they resented this or not, as they never did say a thing. After they read this book I will find out, I sincerely hope that we did not cause any friction or hardship between them, if we did, I am truly sorry. I love both of them so very much; there just is not enough or the right words to express it.

They arranged for their reception to be at a hall with someone we knew and it did cost a lot less. Arrangements were made for a catered Ukrainian meal. Most of all I would be making Tina's Wedding Dress along with her attendants dresses. It was wonderful and I loved every minute working on the dresses, "love" went into every stitch and bead. This Wedding is instilled in my mind and heart forever. Tina's Wedding Dress had a train with lovely bead work, a veil that was trimmed with a single strand of pearls along the whole edge.

Her Bridesmaids and Matron of Honour wore burgundy satin dresses trimmed with burgundy sequins and seed beads along the bodice. There was just enough on each dress that caught the light and shimmered. The Flower Girl was in a medium pink satin dress, this little girl was Tina's sister; they were just beautiful. The Groom wore a black tuxedo and all the Ushers and Best Man wore light grey tuxedos.

We did have a sad time before the Wedding though. Fred's best friend and to be Best Man John had a brain aneurysm. He was kept on life support until his Mother decided to follow the instructions on John's drivers' license. John's organs and eyes were to be donated to those who needed them the most. I did help his Mother to make that decision. I talked to her about how important it was not to have Johns' passing a complete waste by helping others to live and see. I made her feel Johns' face to see how very hot his skin was; there was no way that his brain could survive that heat. The medical staff told her that there was no brain activity at that time; she seemed to believe that the brain could return to normal. It was really hard for her to understand that once lost, there is no more. If they had kept him on life support he could only survive a short time before his organs would start shutting down. If that did happen, it would render his organs useless for transplantation. It was then that Johns' Mother realized the outcome of her Son and let him go.

Once this was all taken care of, Fred had to make a decision as to whether to postpone his Wedding or would John want them to go ahead. We all sat down and talked about it and it was decided that John would want Fred to go ahead and get married. The next thing that had to be decided on was; who would be Fred's Best Man. Since he had another best friend, the decision was made that Albert would do the honour, it was a natural decision. John would have agreed with Fred, believe me, that young man will never be forgotten he is in our hearts forever. Those two, Fred and John, were more like brothers than just best friends; they enjoyed and agreed on most of what they did with each other.

When July 18th. 1988 came along, it was truly a day to remember; there were many good things happening. Some were not so good, it was mostly good though and one was even very funny. Fred had rented a Van to take care of all the members of the family to get to and from the Wedding and the Reception. Well, the unbelievable did happen; Jim and I were left in front of the Church by the driver. Fred did realize we were not there and sent the Van back for us; he was really embarrassed by it. He need not have been embarrassed by this incident, as people are only human and mistakes are made all the time. I have had many a laugh over the incident; there was just too much excitement.

After the reception, Fred and Tina went to a Hotel for the night and returned in the morning to their place for the Bridal Breakfast. After that they were off on their Honeymoon in Florida, it was just super for them. I am glad they were able to go as they should never miss the Honeymoon, if you do, you will never get another chance.

After many nights of talking to Ted on the phone over the years, he decided not to call me on December 22nd. 1988. He called his Psychiatrist, psychiatric Nurse and his case worker; none of them were in town as they were away on Christmas Holidays. He should have known where each of them would be but in his state of mind, it was just not logical. Instead of calling me later, he called the Police. It was early in the morning of the 23rd. of December, after mixing his medications with alcohol; he lost control of his faculties. When the Police knocked on the door, he panicked and promptly hung himself off his balcony at his apartment block.

At 6:30 a.m. there was a knock at our door. I was expecting my milkman to pay him for our months' milk supply. When I opened the door and saw that two very young Policemen were standing there, I instantly knew why they had come. This was what I had been dreading yet expecting, after all the time talking to him and sincerely hoping I could prevent it. The Policeman spoke to me in a very low voice and asked if we would come to the hospital to identify our Son. I invited them in and went to wake Jim up; we dressed and went with the Policemen to the hospital. That was truly harrowing for us that morning. We identified our Son and said our goodbyes; we were then given Ted's jewellery and apartment keys and driven back home. Later that same day, Fred and Tina joined us and helped clean out the apartment. We moved all the furniture and Ted's possessions, arranged to have his car removed to our property; then turned the keys over to the Caretaker. Ted had written down and told us face to face many times that he did not want a funeral. He wanted to be cremated and his ashes to be spread free, this we did for him. What had me amazed was how little there was to prove he even lived. A few identification cards, a car, a lot of junk, some art, music and clothes that were no longer salvageable, most were in the garbage.

Even at that, Jim had managed to make the whole thing a living hell; this is something that will forever be a pain in my heart. Thank goodness that Ted left his life insurance to Fred as the beneficiary; this gave them a chance to purchase their own home. I remember borrowing the money from the Credit Union to get the funds moving on Fred and Tina's new home. When he received the insurance, which was a short time later, the loan was completely paid back; I think I have that right. Since I first wrote this, Fred has told me that I was right about how this was done. It still does not matter, either way; Fred and Tina still bought the home they wanted.

The upheaval that Jim caused over the car, it was something I would rather forget but since it is part of my life, it is now in this book. Jim said that Fred was taking everything and he should not receive the car too. I believe that Jim was angry once again because he thought he was being short changed, that was ridiculous. There was no talking to him about it. I expected nothing and why should I receive something, I just did not understand Jims' way of thinking at all. Of course I am a giving person not a taker. To top this off, Jim made me hire a lawyer to take care of Ted's estate; that was where all the funeral money went. I could and would have done a better job at less money and have all of Ted's debts paid off. This is the kind of thing that happens when a mate feels that the other is incompetent and stupid. We paid for the cremation out of our own pockets; most of the burial money was to pay the Lawyer. As for the Insurance, I am ever so glad that it went to Fred; I really believe that if Jim had received it, it would have been blown on the lotteries. That was what de did with his own insurance when he cashed that in.

Chapter Thirteen

At Christmas 1989, Jim managed to make more hell for Fred, Tina and I. He picked an argument with them in their own home, which in my estimation he had no right to do. It was once again during and over a card game. That was the time that all card games and games of any kind ceased for me. I had enough of his making up his own rules and picking arguments over them after and during the game. This was truly hell; it is hard to put it out of my mind and heart because this kind of thing caused much pain for everyone.

The whole year of 1990 was pure hell for me; I missed my Son and Daughter-in-law so very much. Jim would not give an inch nor would he ever admit that what happened was even remotely his fault. I pleaded with him so many times, but he would have none of it. I know his mind worked in terrible ways but it was truly hard to take. It was only because I was watching a slow deterioration of my Husbands body and mind that I stayed with him, I'm not a quitter.

Besides that, believe it or not, I loved him dearly, go figure, a true glutton for punishment. To top it, I am my own worst enemy; we all are in some way or another. I also knew that he needed help, as his wife only I could care for him. No matter how small or how long a care he might need, no one could ever put up with him like I did. Let me tell you, it was a long hard job to care for someone you have no idea on how much they will need.

My Husband had to have all of his teeth extracted as they were really in a very poor and painful condition. He went into hospital to prepare for the extractions; he was refused by the Heart Specialist. It was necessary to go through a barrage of tests to bring his blood pressure and heart to a controllable point in order to operate on his mouth. After a couple of months, they gave him a clean bill of health to go ahead; this time the anaesthesiest refused to take a chance on him. They sent him to a different hospital and he saw another anaesthesiest. This new Doctor gave the go ahead on the removal of his teeth, arrangements were made and his teeth were all removed.

It was two weeks later that he started to go to a Denturist, it took a while but it was all done. I disagreed with the waiting to put in his dentures that was because they would always be irritating and painful. He could not and would not be able to take that kind of pain; his threshold for pain was very low. I told him that he would probably not wear them for very long and eventually would not wear them at all, unfortunately, I was right. Those plates are still in a container, they have been there for years now, fifteen years to be exact.

On our next Doctor's appointment, they found a

growth on Jim's right lung. The Doctor said he would have to keep an eye on it. They also gave him some new pain medication. It was at this time that they told Jim that he has Crohns disease, a very painful disease of the bowels. It layers the bowels with scar tissue like a fish scale until it builds up and blocks it off. When this happens the area has to be removed as the patient does not get any nutrition. The bowel just could not absorb anything, he lost his strength through this. .

After treating Jim for ulcers and gastroenteritis they have changed it to Crohns, what a bummer. It was shortly after this that he ended up in hospital again with another blockage, this time it was for a longer period of time, one month to be exact. This time a special test called a colonoscopy was done and they told him that his bowels were in a very irritated state. It would be just a matter of time before he would have to be operated on.

He did leave the hospital, very angry because he thought he should have gone home long before. They had fed him such a bland and nearly all liquid diet. It was the last day that they finally allowed him to have ground up food. That not only looked but tasted terrible; I know because I tasted it, it just was not worth the time spent in cooking it.

When I took him home, I looked up a diet for him and found something more palliative and soft; he really did enjoy my cooking. It took a while but I did get it down pat where he had not trouble chewing or swallowing his food, of course, everything was over cooked, it had to be. Just so he could get full nutrition from his food, I steamed most of it so that nothing would be lost and still tasted fairly good. It just amazed me at how much he had to avoid, if he did not, he would be in excruciating pain for trying something different. He was in a constant state of diarrhea and that is what made him lose his nutrients too fast and lose weight also. It was during these times that he sometimes went into a state of absolute confusion; it was a long time before I found out why.

On our next Doctors' visit, Jim was told that he had to see a surgeon over the growth in his lung, it had to be removed. They first sent him for a biopsy on the area, when the results came back it was confirmed that it had to be removed. All the running around with the medical papers again and he was admitted to hospital, it was supposed to be for only ten days. Both of us let the Surgeon know that Jim had Crohns disease; because of it, he had little or no control of his bodily function when unconscious. If Jim was to be unconscious; he had to be diapered, this was a natural precaution to be taken.

The trouble was that the Surgeon chose not to pay attention to our warning and went ahead and operated on Jim without a diaper. Of course you know what could happen did happen. The area in the operating room was no longer sterile; it was full of E-Coli-E. Apparently we carry this dreadful bacterium in our bodies but it remains dormant until it hits the air.

The Surgeon finished the operation under these circumstances and within two days, there was a full blown infection in the area. The Nurses told the Surgeon, he chose to ignore them also; when I seen it I told the Doctor there was an infection there. The arrogant Surgeon said: "None of my operations ever become infected, there is no infection there." I told him: "I have brought up three Sons and I know infection when I see it."

As it turned out, the infection made Jim incoherent and out of reality for ten days. He hallucinated all during that time and made very little sense when talking to us. Jim was put under quarantine and I had to wear a hat, gown, mask and rubber gloves while visiting him. This was so that I would not carry the bacteria out of the room and spread it through the hospital. They took blood several times a day to watch how the massive doses of antibiotics were doing.

I believe that one of oldest medications against bacteria was the only one that actually worked; it eventually cleared the infection from Jim's body. He had to be debraided three times, that is, he was operated on again until all of the infection was cleaned out of the area. They never closed the wound up until it was all clear. They had to take the muscle from the right front rib cage and placed into the right shoulder. If they did not do this, he would not have had the use of his right arm. The infection had totally destroyed that muscle in his shoulder, which is why this had to be done. Jim had some pain in his shoulder after but did have the use of his arm.

During this time Jim found out that they had broken a couple of his ribs and they did not mend properly. This caused much pain over the years, actually the pain never really went away and no medication ever helped to numb the area; Jim found no comfort from pain. He almost died that time and all because of the "arrogance" of a Surgeon who obviously thought he was the best. He still thinks he is the best and so do a lot of other Doctors whom I have great respect for; they did not have to go under his knife though.

It took a long time for Jim to recover from this operation and I do not think he ever really did. As it turned out, the growth was cut away but was lost during the operation; what kind of Surgeon is he? I would not wish this person on my worst enemy if I had one; come to think of it I have, and the enemy is that Surgeon.

This is a warning for the ill, watch out everyone; "hell" is out there just waiting to knock on your door look out for you "backsides." Someone could take a nip out of you in some way or another. I am sorry that I cannot tell you his name as I want my book published; there are rules I must follow or I could be sued. It would not be worth while for me to cause myself even more problems; I have had enough in my life time.

The only good thing that came out of this was Jim being reunited with Fred and Tina; this was all that I ever really wanted all along. The reason he did, is not only did he love them both but, he did not want to die with this anger hanging over his head. As it turned out everything was settled for him. He did not apologize though and he should have, he probably knew he was wrong, at least I hope he did.

I took Jim home after that and things were okay for a while, that is until there was another onset of a seizure, I saw it coming, always did. I took to warning anyone about it if they planned to come over as I did not want them to go through the mouth except me. The awful part of it was, he was so unpredictable and rarely remembered what he said, this way he had caused a lot of pain to others. If he ever remembered what he said, I knew it was a deliberate act on his part.

On June 13th, 1994 we received a phone call from Jim's Sister; his Mother had passed away in hospital. His Mother was in hospital to receive a pace maker as her heart would sometimes not beat properly. This particular day she was going to go out to play bingo and they had left her sitting at the edge of her bed. They turned their backs looking for Mom's shoes and over she went onto the floor. There was a severe brain injury and she did not survive it, she was ninety-one years old. Jim was truly shaken by the news and was very upset that he would not be able to attend her funeral; he was not allowed to travel.

He would spend money like water when it came to lotteries but me needing a new coat or boots, no way, what I had was good enough for another year. My last two winter coats were purchased by me from my own pension money. The only way that he would pay for those two things is if they were like old rags and held no warmth. Even then, he would hesitate, that went equally for him as well as me. He never wanted to spend money on anything unless it was the lottery; his priorities were a little messed up don't you think? If I had to buy clothing for him or I before my pension came into being, he just would have to do without his scratch tickets. When this happened he would get angry and mouth off even more often as he was bored and itching for a scratch ticket. At this time, it was pure hell for me; his mouth could be very venomous.

One day Jim was having a lot of pain and could not eat anything. His Doctor was away and his second in command had to take Jim into hospital and operate on him. They had to remove about half of his intestinal tract, which was both the large and small bowel along with his gallbladder and appendix. Everything they had removed was full of Crohns. He remained in hospital for about two months that time. It took that long to be able to eat normal food and not lose all of his nutrition too fast. Oh that operation did not stop the blockages; it only happened that much more frequently as the bowels were now short. It is called short bowel syndrome and the pain was way out of this world at times.

It was my birthday on December 14th. 1995 Fred and Tina came over to give me a birthday card, or so I had thought. Well, we were all sitting around the living room talking when they said: "We are going to have a Baby!" I had thought that they were just fooling me again as they said the same thing when they adopted a new kitten or puppy. I said: "Oh sure, what is it this time, a new puppy?" They said: "No it is for real this time," boy this almost blew our minds. What a Birthday gift for me, none other would do. Finding out we were going to be Grandparents was absolutely the greatest. We also asked when the baby was due and we were told in August 1996. That winter I was kept busy making baby things for the new little one; this also helped me not to worry over Tina. It sure was nice to be able to do some knitting, crocheting and sewing again without being yelled at, what a marvellous experience.

On the next three month visit with our Doctor, we found that he had left town and went to the United States, this was without letting his patients know. We found that our new Doctor was a "pip squeak" who also had a "God" complex; only, we did not know it at that time. We decided between us that we would give him a chance; on hindsight it was the biggest mistake we ever made. Never should have accepted him as a replacement Physician. At that time it was very difficult to find a new Doctor; and the problem was that my Husband being in such poor health, needed someone to take care of him right away. Anyway this new Physician sent us up to the hospital to get blood tests, x-rays and a urinalysis. At the top of the hill Jim lost his footing and took a fall, pulled my left arm so hard that it caused damage to my shoulder. You see, Jim could not walk without some kind of assistance, mainly holding onto my arm. His personal pride or ego prevented him from using a cane or a walker.

For the next three months, I went to physiotherapy three days a week except on a holiday week, all that care and my left arm is still useless. Of course Jim did not want me to go to therapy as it took time away from him; he considered it a waste of time. I wanted to go and give myself a chance to return the arm to normal. While having hot compresses put on the shoulder, it did okay but as soon as it cooled off, the arm returned to being stiff. Even now I still get a lot of pain and find that putting on a back loading bra that I need assistance, front loading is okay. Most times I have great difficulty reaching behind me to dress and cannot lift that arm above my shoulder. It was a bummer I know but had learned to live with it, I always find a way to get around something that is truly difficult to do.

This injury is now a permanent disability and I have forgiven Jim for leaving me with it. At the very first it made me angry, if he had of used a cane or a walker I would not be in this pain or have trouble using my arm. The anger is long gone, once the injury took place it was a done deal. There just was no sense to feeling sorry for myself or crying over it, taking care of the arm and learning to do what I could was more important. The only reason I did mention this in my book is to show that sometimes no matter how much care or exercise you have, the problem is not solved. One has to adapt to the circumstances or they are lost; there is arthritis in that shoulder now. I have to take medication for it and sometimes it helps reduce the pain, it is now part of my life. There is absolutely nothing that will change it. An occasional rub down does relieve some of the pain which makes it a little more tolerable.

It was August 11th. 1996 when we received a phone call from our son Fred, he was at the hospital. Apparently Fred and Tina were out shopping at one of the malls, when Tina started to feel poorly. He called the hospital and they told him to bring Tina in, he did so and then called us. He said he was going to take her home as it was a false alarm. Not so. While on the phone with us they had taken her to the delivery room. After he had hung up, we thought that they had returned home. A little later on we received another call from Fred. We had a brand new Grandson and his name is Bradley James, BJ for short, what a beautiful child. When we seen BJ, we told them that he looks just like Fred did when we received him at six days old, what a glorious memory. There were a few times that we actually were given the opportunity to baby sit, which was a real challenge again. It allowed us to bond with Bradley; it was a wonderful time we spent together.

Just before Christmas that year, Jim had another blockage in the bowels, this time though, it was not as bad. It cleared up quickly, only ten days in hospital and he was able to return home again. It turned out to be not a bad Christmas that year, just had to watch what I fed him. There were some more no-no's in his diet; slowly his food intake and medications had to be re-adjusted to his intestinal problems.

In the year 1997, there were a few more trips to the hospital over intestinal blockages; some took quite a while to clear. That pump is not an ideal thing to be attached to for days and all you may have is ice chips once in a while. Jim was also attached to an IV of course, that is where he received his nutrition and all of his medications.

There were many outbursts of anger from Jim. One day he once again accused me of fooling around but that stemmed from his Brothers lies that I was having affairs at the SPA. This time he made the accusations and actually laughed at me when he made me cry. That hurt like crazy and it made me sick to see that he thought it was so funny. I do know for a fact that he knew what he was doing this time, he was just being plain mean and spiteful. I went for a long walk to clear my head and get of the anger; it just was not easy to do.

On returning home I said absolutely nothing to him for days, it had to be that way as the anger would only flare up again. Those were many rough days for me. The reason I am writing about it is to show that this is a really serious problem. Also to let those who are in the same situation as I was in know that it never goes away. Please think long and hard about what situation you are in; do not stay if you can get away, things will never change and it is definitely mean. They do mean it when they do this and they definitely do not love you, you are their punching bag or verbal kicks.

On June 23rd. 1998 I received a phone call from my sister Irene informing me that my Father had passed away. He was 93 years old and had dementia, he will be dearly missed by everyone.

At Christmas time in 1998, our Son Fred took a job change with the same company; it required him to move to Sudbury, Ontario. They spent Christmas with us and we all had a wonderful time together, Bradley was simply precious. He loved to play dump truck with all my spools of thread and other safe sewing objects. What a great time Bradley had. He managed to unravel and tangle my thread from the spools and bobbins. Jim was upset over it, it just did not bother me at all and I took some precious pictures of the whole incident. Since it was my things and it did not bother me, why should anyone else become angry or upset? Later on I spent hours untangling the thread. It just made me smile every time I thought of my Grandson playing with the thread, thimbles and bobbins. To me, it was a great day all around and ever so precious and funny. Bradley also loved garlic sausage, pickles and cheese; he was constantly eating all that day. He just loved to watch Grandma in the kitchen putting everything out. Bradley never reached on the table unless I told him it was okay, he was very good that way.

In January 1999 we had Bradley and his two little dogs for a full day; one was a Lhasa apso and the other one was a Schi Tzu. Fred and Tina were busy packing and loading up all their possessions into a truck and into the van for their move to Sudbury. Bradley and Grandma walked the dogs many, many times that day; it was very cold out. A super day for both of us, I shall cherish and remember it. Anyway they did find a nice little place to rent and found it ever so peaceful. It is a great place to bring up children as there is very little traffic, what there is, all go slowly through the neighbourhood. Their Landlords were an elderly couple and they became good friends with them.

There were many ups and downs that year for us. A few hospital stays over the intestinal problem. There were many rough times over Jim's mouth also; fortunately Fred was now away from it all this time. Not so for Daniel, he "hung tough" so to speak and stayed here for me. I will never regret the adoption of our two Sons as they gave me the stability when the going was rough. Thank "God" for children, they are often a Mother's life saver, they sure were for me. It was this way many, many times in our marriage; my children were my life and still are along with my Grandsons now.

Jim, Daniel and I went to a very nice restaurant on December 24th. 1999 to celebrate our Fortieth Wedding Anniversary, it was great. We even brought home our dinners for the evening as this restaurant was closed by 1:00 p.m. on Christmas Eve. Each of us chose completely different meals to take home as we did not want the same as at lunch, the meals were delicious.

Two days later, I made my Husband hot chicken noodle soup for lunch. The reason it was hot, he would not eat it any other way. He was not feeling too well that day and I should have known what was about to happen. Guess that I was too tired that day and let down my guard on the whole situation. Jim had decided to have his lunch sitting at the edge of the bed; I brought him his soup and walked away. As I reached the kitchen which was only a few steps away, there was a rattle of a cup and bowl. This told me that he was having a seizure and that I had to return to help him. It was then that I saw Jim had spilled the hot soup all over him and was standing trying to brush off the noodles from his clothes. He was not aware what was happening, this took place when he was having a mini-seizure.

As he came out of the seizure, I called for a taxi and immediately took Jim to the hospital. When we arrived, they took us into an examining room, immediately poured ice cold sterile water on the burns. After that they placed ice packs on the burns, it helped kill the pain right away. Because of it being the weekend and a holiday week to boot, the hospital emergency was extra busy with many seriously ill people. Plus all the usual drunks who got hurt, some were with sprains and broken bones; one even had stab wounds and actually survived the ordeal. See, I still believe our Lord is watching over us at all times. We ended up waiting for a long time as others were even in worse condition and had to be cared for first. Once our turn came up, they did a very good job. We were told to go home and return in two days, we did just that and once again had to wait hours. The emergency room is no place to have to wait, too many angry people. Of course, if the staff just let them know once in a while, that these patients are not forgotten, it would really go a long way. Then again, maybe not, some are angry all of the time and nothing would suffice.

On the Monday when we returned to the hospital once again, Jim was placed in an examining room, who says that is quicker? No it is not, believe it, we waited for at least five hours before a Doctor stopped in to examine Jim. It was a Doctor who was just passing by and had a quick look. He had walked about five steps, turned around and came in; he seen something from a distance that no one noticed up close. This Doctor had noticed that Jim had third degree burns in some areas; this is when the skin turns absolutely white surrounded by very red areas. He called for a surgeon who specialized in taking care of burns and in skin grafting. When she examined Jim, she bandaged him up, told us to return at 7:00 a.m. the next morning; she would arrange for his admittance and the operation.

Well, we did go home and returned to the hospital at 6:45 a.m. the next morning. That day, I stayed with Jim until 6:00 p.m., he still had not been taken care of. I returned home to take care of Daniel and me, cooked us our dinner and sat down to relax. At about 10:00 p.m. Jim phoned me and told me that he was still sitting in the waiting room. He had received no acknowledgement whatever, nothing to eat or drink and none of his medications. After I hung up the phone, I put in a call to the hospital and asked for the Surgeon by name. When my call was put through, I asked her what was up in regards to my Husband and his burns. She told me that he had not shown up, I said: "What do you mean, didn't show, I brought him to the hospital before 7:00 a.m. and the he was still there. He has been there all the time and has not even received so much as a drink of water." Guess I stirred up a "hornet's nest" as Jim was immediately taken upstairs and not only did he receive his medications but some much needed water. No food was given though as he was to be operated on early the next morning. When in the operating room, skin was taken from his right thigh and transplanted to the area where the third degree burns were. Not only were there burns on his tummy, but his wrists and right hand had some too, it was all very painful.

After ten days in hospital, they sent Jim home with me but not before I received instructions on how to care for his burns. There was a very patient and qualified nurse with the same first name as mine. She showed me how to take care of the burns and even had me do the changing of the bandages in front of her. Of course I was extremely slow, that made it even more painful for Jim. The job I did, though slow, was done right according to the nurse. She filled two large garbage bags with plenty of extra bandages, sterile water, gauze wraps, paper tape and sterile bandage trays with scissors and rubber gloves. This was all to enable me to do the job right without extra cost. It took a little while for me to do it quicker but I succeeded, even at that there was a lot of pain.

I will never forget the experience and do not ever wish to take care of another patient with a burn; it was pure hell for me. Of course, if it was necessary to do this for Daniel or myself, I would. Jim's mouth was wicked, that was one of the worst times for me, and I truly felt incompetent at doing the job at that time. His degradation of me at that time only made it even more painful for him; this was because I was always nervous.

He obviously did not think that his badgering made me very upset and caused me to do things even slower and more painful. He kept me on a constant move, jumping to his every beck and call all through it. It took a while, but I did survive the experience and so did he, or should I call it an ordeal? Am at a loss as to how I managed to survive. I hope and pray that no one else has to experience this in their life time. By that I mean, the cruelty of mouth by a spouse.

Anyway, hot soup was never given to Jim again unless he was sitting at the table. Even if he is not feeling well, all eats were now eaten at the table, no more burns. The other thing is Jim was told if he had to go outside, he must be fully covered at all times as the sun could and would burn his skin very quickly.

In the spring of that year, Jim decided to put in a garden of tomatoes and flowers, it had been years since he did any gardening. It was equally as long since he felt like doing any, what a marvellous time that was; he was actually civil to me. That I did understand because he had denied me so much of what I loved to do.

The crop of tomatoes was fabulous, we gave a lot away and the rest I put up in heavy plastic bags and froze them. We gave away a lot to our friend Laura at the corner store, she really was very grateful for that. It was a few years earlier that we welcomed her and her family to the neighbourhood. From then on, Laura and I have been fast friends and will continue to be for the rest of my life, she is one super person. They are Filipino; I also found most people from her race are just like her, easy to love.

What a lovely tomato sauce I made for Italian Spaghetti, all from scratch, it was worth every effort. That was the time that I had received a lot of compliments from Jim. What a surprise it was to me, I of all people did understand why.

You see, when Jim decided to do something he loved to do, his personality did a complete reversal. All he had to do was make up his mind, put in the effort and decide that it was what he really wanted. He should have done it more often and his life would have improved also, not to mention mine. When you lose so much of your own personality, as well as the time, you do not realize what is happening to you.

Near fall time that year, we received a phone call from our son Fred; he informed us that they were expecting their second child in April 2000. That was when Jim actually suggested that I go to Fred's for a holiday at the time near the birth of our second Grandchild.

I took Jim up on the offer and actually did get to use my train pass for the first time in almost twenty-one years. I left Winnipeg to go to Sudbury on April 1st. 2000 and arrived the next day; I stayed for three whole weeks. It was a marvellous time for me, though there were times that Bradley was rough on Grandma and Mommy. We, meaning Bradley and I, walked to and from the playground quite a few times. We would play together with the stationary backhoe, play in the sand, climb monkey bars and slide down the slides. After we were finished at the play ground I would take Bradley to have hot chocolate and chips, we really enjoyed that. Doing this together allowed Tina to have a break, when we did go, we were gone for at least two hours. The only trouble was, I did not bring my winter coat with me and it was so cold there all the time except for the last couple of days. This was one lesson I learned, if going to go for a visit, make sure that my clothes are warm enough.

When the 18th. of August came around, Tina's Doctor wanted her to come into hospital as they were going to induce the birth of Gregory. Fred took Tina to the hospital and while there; the Doctor had noticed that the umbilical cord was wrapped around the baby's neck. Without so much as a "by your leave" to Fred, they whisked Tina to the operating room and gave her a caesarean section. When Fred heard the cry, he knew it was his little boy Gregory William who was just born. I really received the chance to spend a few days with Gregory before I had to return home again. When I arrived home, Jim was very glad to see me; he apparently missed me a lot. That unfortunately lasted only for a little while, slowly but surely, the mouth started again, it always did. Once Jim got used to me again, the old angers came back and he expected me to jump to his every call. If I did not move fast enough, the mouth with the bad language and names were right there as if I had never left. At least while away, Daniel never received the mouth like that, they apparently got along most of the time, at least Daniel never said anything. He has since confirmed that Jim had been very compatible with Daniel, I am truly glad to hear that.

After Christmas 2000, Jim's personality took another turn for the worse; the rages were getting closer together. I had to watch when I went out and get home in good time, did not dare to be any later than usual. Sometimes it had nothing to do with what I had done or had to do, there were times that the bus would take off early. When that happened I would have to explain why and even then, Jim did not believe what I said. There were times when I took Daniel shopping with me just so the suspicions would stop. It worked and gave me a little extra time away without rushing. Daniel saved me a lot of problems, even though he hated to go shopping, he would go with me just to keep peace in the house. There were times that the intestinal problems robbed Jim of his nutrition. This caused Jim's mental capacity to deteriorate, and it did not matter if Daniel went shopping with me then or not, the rages would bloom into arguments.

In December 2001 Jim had another problem over his bowels, he acquired an allergy to his pain medication, it caused bleeding and sent him into hospital again. This time, he had severe diarrhea and bleeding in the intestinal tract, he refused the pain medication much to the chagrin of our Doctor. That little "twerp" yelled at Jim in the middle of the room in front of four other patients and said he had to take the medication. Jim would not and did not ever take it again; he also never had any bleeding in his intestinal tract again. This same Doctor tried to get me to persuade Jim to take that medication, I would not do so. The bleeding and severe pain occurred each time; to me that was enough as it was causing more problems than it was helping. The Physician tried to lay a guilt trip on me; he told me that it was my entire fault that Jim was so ill. He said I was actually killing him, I had better smarten up or he would not last long. You know, that simply was not true, Jim's illness had nothing to do with what I did or was doing. At least I found solutions to help ease Jim's pain and help him retain most of his nutrition. It was more that what that Doctor did; he never suggested any diets for Jim.

Anyway I returned to Jim and asked him if he was game to going home; he said yes. After Jim signed himself out, we were met at the elevator by a man that he thought was a marriage councillor. I said: "Come on Dad, this man is a Psychiatrist and he is here to persuade us to stay." No way, we were going home and never would see that Doctor we had ever again. I wish that could have been true, we did see him at the hospital many times but not as our Physician, thank goodness. We never did speak to him again. After I took Jim downstairs with a wheelchair, I phoned for a cab and we returned home. At the beginning of the week, I went Doctor hunting.

Chapter Fifteen

In the first week of January 2002, I found a Doctor who was close to our home and was easy to get to by bus. Well, nothing is ever as easy as it seems, there is always something that gets in the way; that is all part of life. The new Doctor told us that he did not like Jim's blood work up and refused to take care of him. Of course Jim did not like that and swore at him that clinched him not being our Doctor. Up to that time there was a possibility; Jim should have kept his mouth shut. We found out later that it did not matter what Jim had said, that Doctor was already influenced by our former Physician. We did find another Doctor but before we went to see him, I contacted the Physicians and Surgeons group requesting that they put a stop to any interference by him. They asked if we wanted to press charges and I told them only if he interfered again, he did not. Our newest Doctor turned out to be the best we ever had and I will not change to another one for anything in the world. Of course if he retires, than I will have no choice but my Doctor promised to put me in another good Physicians hands. All I can say is thank goodness that we were lucky this time.

During 2002, our new Doctor made sure that Jim had top care, he was first sent to see a Cardiologist who changed his heart and blood pressure medications. This was necessary as Jim's blood pressure did a complete reversal. Sometime during the wait for a new Doctor,

Jim's blood pressure dropped and was causing a lot of problems. His heart was weaker and could not pump the fluid from his legs, that fluid is called edema. It is an accumulation of serous fluid in a serous cavity. This is an indication of poor heart output and it continued right up into his groin and up under his rib cage.

They put Jim on some extra diuretics and they actually worked for a while. His mental capacity deteriorated also, they took a blood test for his albumen level; it was very low. Our Doctor put him back into hospital for the transfusions of albumen; this is from whole blood. It is a protein which helps keep your mind alert; without it you are a lost soul. After a few days and a few transfusions, Jim's mental capacity started to return so they sent him home once again. At home I tried to find a way to help him to get all his proteins through his food and to keep it. Sometimes that was hard to do as diarrhea is the culprit that makes one lose it fast, often it is a losing battle but I tried anyway, never gave up.

After his hospital trip, he would be okay for a few months, a true respite for Daniel and me. As you can see, there were times that he really had no control over his actions. This always stayed in the back of my mind; believe that I realized it and handled the situation just the right way. Yes I do know it is no excuse for abuse, but at that time you could not tell me that. My son Fred tried to tell me what was happening, but I just did not see it or, was it believed it? I know that I was in full denial and that was really unfortunate. If the denial was realized by me, my Doctor would have given me the help that was needed; he did obtain the help for me later. Anyway, I know now, that is why I am writing this book; it is a good experience as well as therapy.

In 2003, Jim's Crohns showed its ugly face again, and it was taking all of his nutrition from his body. He could not control his bowels at all and there came a time that he had to be diapered. His legs needed constant attention, the bandages that had to be used cost a fortune and they were not covered by our Health Insurance when at home. It was truly hard to budget with so much need; I did find a way to ease the pressure. It meant going around our City to purchase the bandages. Let me tell you, having a telephone .made it even easier as then it cut down on the useless trips. During that time, I must have been to every store and drugstore that had a sale just to save a little money, it was tough going. It cost at least $150.00 per week for bandages and the prescription cream; sometimes it cost more when I had to pay the full price. This never left much to live on; it was the only way that I could make ends meet. To top it all, the odour from the drainage of the legs was horrendous, it smelled just like urine. No spray would kill the odour, no disinfectant would either. This went on for quite a while; he did get a reprieve from it. The bandaging and diuretics finally did their job; it also cut down the pain.

The problem was it only lasted for a short while. Jim's body got used to the diuretics and then the madness started all over again; a vicious circle. His mental capacity was also deteriorating at this time; he was constantly yelling in pain. I had trouble keeping up with everything that was needed, it is really hard to see all this happening to someone, and often you feel useless.

One day, he started throwing up bile, and had to be put into hospital once again. While in hospital, he contracted a serious infectious bacterium, it was called "edificial." The person is under quarantine because it can be carried throughout the hospital; all the staff and patients can come down with it, what a mess that would be. When visiting, I had to wear a gown, cap, mask and rubber gloves, no exception; I was told if I did not do so, I would be banned. Naturally, I behaved myself and wore the items, anything so as not to make someone else ill.

It was in July that they had to operate on his intestinal tract again, there was only a slit opening in the bowels and it was full of Crohns. All during this time, it was harrowing for us; Jim was in so much pain and wanted me with him all the time. I was there seven days a week from 11:00 a.m. to 8:00 p.m., I finally had to put a stop to it. I had to cut back the amount of days as well as the hours; it was just too stressful for me. During that time Jim had many blood transfusions of whole blood as well as albumen. There were times that Jim did not know where he was and was hallucinating; he would see animals and even one of his Grandsons.

At the advice of our Doctor, I seen and talked to the Social Worker as well as the Pastor of the hospital, they helped me out tremendously. I had lost forty-six pounds in less than a month; the nurses were worried about me. They told me I was burning out and they were right, I had to take better care of myself. I would guess that my Doctor also recognized my problems or he would not have sent me to the Social Worker. Anyway, when I took Jim to hospital that time, I weighed in at 211 pounds and wore a size 22. At the time that I seen the Social Worker I had to buy myself new clothes. I went down to 165 pounds and wore a size 16; it had just melted off me. One day I got the sweet tooth and ate a whole box of chocolates in a couple of days, I dropped 10 pounds. Not many people can claim this happened to them; it was just weird how the stress stripped the pounds off. What was even stranger, it was lost evenly all through the body. Right now, today that is, I am 150 pounds and a size 10 petite; do not know where it has all gone as I did and do not diet. I have never been a size 10; it is costing me money for clothes like never before, I really look good though. My suggestion to everyone is, do not lose weight this way, it is just too drastic.

Our Doctor had arranged for Jim to see and talk

to a Psychiatrist while in hospital, he did not want to see the man; he saw no problem between us. I seen all the problems and these people helped me out, they took good care of me. Jim was in hospital a total of eight months this time and they suggested that he go into a nursing home. I should have put him there but, I listened to Jim's begging and let him talk me into taking him home.

In April 2004 he came home for the last time, I thought that I could handle him once more. I was wrong; hear that everyone, I was WRONG! The Social Worker, Psychiatrist, Preacher as well as our Doctor were right; I just could not handle Jim any longer.

Jim was home for three weeks when he started losing it once more and really gave me a lot of trouble. The next three weeks were pure hell. One day he up and accused me of fooling around. This made me so upset, I cried like crazy, just could not believe he was doing this to me again. Well he was and he knew what he was doing. He started to laugh at me; I just had to go out, almost left him that time. I thought this was my home too as it was in my name; why should I give up my home? It was not much but it was just as much mine as it was his; I earned the right to be here. This time I went for a long walk and returned with a straighter head. I told him: "Why should I leave, it is my home and you are not chasing me away. Let me tell you that you will never get away with those accusations again, and to top it, laugh at me. You just will not get away with it, take my word for it, this is final." After that Jim went down hill steadily, he would not go to sleep and would not let me sleep either. He lost complete control of his bodily functions, even though there was a commode right beside him in the living room, he never made it. What a mess, I literally scrubbed holes in the carpet in order to clean it. All the covers on the couch and chairs were a mess, they had to be stripped and washed.

All during this time, I had a very bad time in trying to keep him clean, especially his legs. I did do it but it was very stressful and I was just too tired. One day I did get him to go to bed, do not know how I managed to persuade him to go; it was a really bad period of time. I tried to get him to eat and he just would not, so figured I had better start keeping track of all his intake and output of liquids and solids. As it turned out, it was a good thing that I did. I had to call the Doctor later and that was when Jim hung the phone on me. The Doctor's wife called me back and asked if everything was okay. I told her what was happening and she told me to take him to hospital right away. When I called for an Ambulance, he hung the phone up on me again. They called me back and asked me how aggressive was my Husband, I told them and they sent the Fire Department first. When they arrived, there were five very large gentlemen to take care of the situation, Jim took one look at them and promptly passed out. Within five minutes the Ambulance arrived, by that time Jim was awake. The Lady paramedic was a little rough on him, he said: "A fine professional you are, you hurt me." The Firemen and Paramedic all laughed, so did I to be truthful. She rolled Jim into a bed sheet and with the help of the Firemen; they carried him into the front room where the gurney was. Jim never did remember that night or even that week at all; it took at least another ten days before he came around.

That was when I told him what happened and how he ended up in hospital once again. He was receiving transfusions of albumen; the difference was he was getting up out of bed as his mental capacity returned. One time he had a mini-seizure while on his feet; he was going to go to the washroom, he had taken a fall. One of the care givers found him on the floor and rang for assistance. When they tried to stand him up they found he could not and placed him back into his bed. They found out after an x-ray that he had broken his right hip and it would have to be operated on. If it was not taken care of, he would not be able to walk again. In some cases even at that the patient is not able to carry his weight. There was an additional problem, his tests came back; Jim once again had the bacterium called "edificial" and was put in quarantine. As for the operation, that had to wait for all the other patients that were scheduled to be operated on done first. Reason, once Jim was operated on; the room had to be fully disinfected in order for no other patient to get the same bacterium.

After the operation, Jim found it very hard to get back on his feet again, after a while he even stopped trying, he was too tired. He often said: "I am trying aren't I Mom?" and equally as often I had to say no he was not, that was because he was just not trying. Other patients who were in the same condition would get up and give it a good effort, not Jim. Doing it his way, Jim ended up being wheelchair bound and in hospital for four months. His lack of effort made it impossible for him to carry his weight on his right leg. The whole situation prevented him from returning home. He was in need of constant care; I could no longer handle that by myself at home. Having someone to come in a couple of hours per day was not good enough either, I needed someone for at least eight hours per day to give me that break. Besides that, our house being over 100 years old; was too old to receive Government assistance for a wheelchair ramp. This was okay by me, sorry, I loved him but I just could not take it anymore, am a human being not a machine. During those six weeks he was home, I found that I was very angry and almost hit him a few times. This was no good and I did not want that at all; he had to go to the nursing home for both of our sakes.

After many discussions together with the Social Worker and the Pastor, some were only with Jim. He realized that I was hurting and that it was he who caused the pain. Even at that, he was still angry over being put into a nursing home. When there, he had everything he ever needed or wanted. I made sure that he had canes to start walking with along with two types of walkers. One had two wheels with skids for indoors and the other had four wheels, a seat and brakes so that he would not go too fast. He never did use any of them. I also purchased a new wheelchair with two types of pads for comfort. It had two sets of foot and leg bracings to be attached when one or the other was needed and most comfortable.

While there I also bought him his own telephone so he could be in touch with me anytime. He had his own television set which was brought from home along with a VCR and a DVD player. There was also a combination radio, tape and CD player for his own entertainment whenever he wished to use them. I bought and put together four storage units for his Videos, CDs, DVDs and all his personal items. He had at least 200 movies there at the nursing home.

After a while I purchased a small refrigerator with a very small freezer in it to keep his perishables in. This was because if he kept them in the general use refrigerator, others helped themselves. Doing this saved many an argument and nothing went missing unless Jim lost or ate it himself. Also I ordered bottled water to be brought in. He did not like tap water, neither do I for that matter, bottled water has a better taste and makes good coffee. He received his daily newspaper and at the beginning of every month, I would give him $90.00 to spend as he pleased. He did lose it a couple of times and I replaced it. I would then put it out of my mind like it was a utility bill, once paid it was gone. Doing it this way stopped my anger that usually swelled up in me. It kept me cool headed and I never lost my temper over money again.

There was a fellow in the nursing home who could come and go as he pleased because he had all his faculties and was there of his own choosing. This gentleman would get the lottery tickets that Jim wanted. Once the money was spent he had to wait until the end of the month to get more, I was not going to back down on that. You would be surprised how cool it kept my head in doing it this way.

While there Jim developed an additional problem, it is called kleptomania. It was up to me to return the items he took as he did not want to give them up. He would pick-up towels, face cloths, diapers of every size and description. He also picked up nail clippers, newspapers and magazines that were not his. These items he would store in garbage bags in his closet or under his bed. At the request of the cleaning staff and the nurses, I would clean out his room once a week, all under protest of course. I would fill two garbage bags with paper and magazines. All the items that were not his and not garbage, I would return to the owners. Every week it would all start over again, it was a viscous circle.

All the time this was taking place at the nursing home, I was trying to clean out the mess here at home. The smell in our mattress from his leaking legs when he was home, took a lot of scrubbing and disinfecting to clean it up. It took many re-scrubbings and disinfections before it finally lost the bad odour. I had to do this as I could not afford a new one, still cannot. Until the bed lost its odour, I slept on the couch. Also was sorting out all the junk at home and driving both the garbage men and recyclers nuts. I am sure they wondered what was going on here. There was a lot to do but could only do a little at a time and on the days I was at home.

All during the time Jim was in the nursing home, I would take him out shopping to the malls all over the City. We went to different ones every other week; we would use the special transit system for handicapped people. In the good spring and summer weather, we would go to the grocery store for cookies and whatever else he might want. This we did twice a week, if it was nice weather he would even buy his ice cream treat. We used the kneeling buses which also had wheelchair ramps to move from one place to another. Jim wanted to go out everyday, this I just could not do; he never realized that my heart could not take all that pushing around everyday of the week. When I did take him out, it would be necessary for me to use the nitro spray as my heart acted up. There were even times that I found it difficult to breathe. At times I would push myself to accommodate Jim. That was when he did notice I was near dropping. If he did not stop the demands, he would kill me. He just could not get along without me and knew it. When we went to the malls, we went for the whole day. We would have lunch together and quite often bought a lot of things to bring back with us. It would be a long day for both of us but he would be happy again.

On our 45th Wedding Anniversary, I again took him to our favourite restaurant. Because it was Christmas Eve, it would close at 1:00 p.m. We would have lunch and bring back a dinner to heat in the microwave later. Yes Daniel met us there and enjoyed the meals too. I always tried to make Jim's life as comfortable and as pleasant as possible, held no grudges. There were times that Jim would bad mouth me; I would just go home without even saying goodbye. It was the only way he understood that he was being a real pain in the backside. Once I did this, he would behave himself for a while and then the mouth would occur again. I would go home without saying goodbye once more. He did not like that one bit; it was the only way that I kept my sanity. After I left, he often would say to the other residents, I do not understand women. Guess I said something that I should not have, it really bothered my wife, cannot remember what it was though. The short memory span was getting shorter as time went on.

Also while in the nursing home, he ended up in the hospital because his albumen level was too low. On one of these occasions, I had a good talk with the hospitals' on duty Physician. This was because he told me that Jim's albumen level was normal. I asked him to go back and check again as Jim did not know me, sure enough, that was the problem. This Doctor never tried to argue with me over Jim again. When he returned to normal it was back to the nursing home. Let me say that I have no regrets whatever when it comes to Jim, I believe that I did the very best for him. I was always there for him, what more can be said, it is not bragging just plain fact. Just do not want anyone to think or say that I was neglectful or non-caring, I was neither, I always made sure he had good medical care whenever needed.

Even at that, there were many arguments; he never liked me to pay attention to other people. It did not matter whether they were male or female as Jim was very possessive of my time. I was often accused of fooling around though I never had the time to do so. Do know if he had thought about it, he would have realized how foolish he was being about that. When I was not with him, I was at home trying to get rid of all the junk he had accumulated over the years. If not doing that, there was shopping, washing and ironing, paying the bills and in general taking care of family needs here at home. Also, all he needed to do was pick up the phone and call me, I was usually home.

Over the years, he saved literally everything, newspapers, fliers, envelopes, utility bills, empty folded Kleenex boxes, you name it, he saved it. He would find a use for it, even crooked nails and pieces of wood. Some were used but basically most of it was just plain garbage. Now you might wonder how many fliers could be accumulated, well, let me tell you. Our son Daniel has been delivering fliers and a weekly newspaper every week for years. Often there would be as many as fifty extra of each flier and the same as the weekly newspaper. Jim would never let them be put into the garbage or the recycling blue boxes when that came into effect.

Why did he save all of this when it could never be used for anything? I do not know! He would drive me around the bend at times as he would never let me touch or dispose of anything. Once in the nursing home, that all changed, thank goodness. At first I got rid of everything except one copy of each newspaper, satellite guide and sports magazines. You would never believe how many folded Kleenex boxes I found; it was enormous, boxes and bags full. Even then, I ended up with twenty-two covered totes; they were the sixty-one litre size. Can you imagine how much space they took? When I first started, everything was in garbage bags and boxes in a room measuring at 8'6" high, by 8'6" wide by 11' long. This room was packed solid, absolutely no space to move around in. There was no time to relax, I was always tired and stressed out, and rarely did I ever watch television, still do not have the time.

When at the nursing home, I would take care of Jim, kept him clean at all times. Changed his bed at least once a week as well as get him out to enjoy some of life. I went through all the bad and grim stuff by becoming very professional about it; did not want him to suffer anymore the he absolutely had to. There were times that it was impossible to take care of his needs without causing pain. There were too many raw and enlarged areas; they were extremely painful when touched. It was the edema that crept up into the groin right up under his rib cage that was causing the pressure pain. I do know that when I did this for Jim; it made it a lot easier on the staff at the nursing home. It was greatly appreciated by them, they have told me so many times with all their thanks. With all of his problems and trouble that he gave me, I still loved him. I just cannot explain it to anyone, is it madness maybe? There were times that I had thoughts of quitting but decided not to, just not a quitter. These are the times that I have paid the price for it in some way or another.

I was very angry and had taken to asking for God's help everyday to control it, to me it was and still is my greatest sin. I know that God is with me and helping me to cope with all that is happening. There were times that I was ridiculed for my beliefs, am just sorry that I could not enjoy my Lord for most of my life. Deep down, I always knew that He was on my side, now know that for sure. Have been reading the Bible daily and also pray to God every night. The few times that I have fallen asleep while praying, I just continued the prayer in the morning when I woke up. Mostly I pray for His help on my temper, to forgive my sins, and for all of my Family and Friends. Also pray for my Sponsored Children and their Families as well as the destitute and starving in the world. I truly believe He is helping everyone as well as me. Now everyone who reads this knows where I am coming from.

On February 6th. one day before Jim's Birthday, I received a call from our Niece informing me that Jim's Sister had passed away. She had a massive coronary, it was very quick. When I told Jim about it he was upset by it and then calmed down. He had wanted to take a trip to Vancouver to see her; I was in the middle of making those arrangements for it. Needless to say, the trip never took place. After that, Jim was getting weaker as time went on, that was when he started asking me to pray for him. I informed him that I already was doing just that, he was in need of God's help and I knew that, I asked Him to take good care of Jim for me. Many times after that he would be very angry and would lash out at me more frequently. Jim would also fall asleep more frequently and my time with him was often quiet, those times were okay.

Jim and I went out on a shopping trip to one of the Malls on Saturday, July 8th. We had lunch together; it was a good day all around, he was very happy over the trip. He had purchased quite a few things that he

wanted and was much like and elated child. This was
not to last for long; before I left him he told me that he
was not feeling too good. He just could not pin point
the problem at all, it made him feel very anxious. The
nurses tried to help him; they took his temperature and
blood pressure, listened to his heart and just could not
find anything wrong. I decided to go home at my usual
time at 5:30 p.m., he was in good hands and thought I
had nothing to worry about.

At approximately 1:30 a.m. on July 9th. Jim
phoned me; he asked if I would be angry if he went to
hospital. I told him of course not, they would probably
take some blood for testing and send him back to the
nursing home. The very last thing that I said to him
was: "By the way, I love you!" I should have known
that there was something wrong right away as he never
wanted to go to hospital; it just did not alert me, think I
must have been too tired.

At 5:30 a.m. that same morning, the night nurse
who Jim always argued with; called me and she was
crying. She told me that Jim had passed away in the
Ambulance before he reached the hospital. I had sat
down on the bed and started to shake, this did not stop
for forty-eight hours, as quickly as it came, it stopped.
It was my Doctor who later told me that his heart was
working only at 15% of its capacity. Jim had a massive
heart attack, it was all over quickly.

Later that day, I had made arrangements to have Jim cremated and as he had wished for, no funeral was to take place. I would later take his ashes to the west coast and spread them over his Parent's graves. On Monday I made arrangements for all the Pension transfers, made sure that the house was put in my name only. I then had my Last Will and Testament made out as well as the Power of Attorney done. This was necessary so that if anything happened to me, my son Daniel would have absolutely no trouble carrying out my wishes. He even knows what nursing home I wished to be placed in if it becomes necessary. If for some reason that I could not cope with life, no ifs ands or buts about it, that nursing home would become my next place of residence. These things were never done by Jim, it was a sore spot with me and I have since forgiven him for his shortcomings.

When it came to his wheelchair and accessories, canes and walkers they all went to an International Organization. This was so that someone who needs this kind of assistance and could not afford it; would receive it without a problem and at no charge. Our local Organizations no longer accept such donations as they have no storage space for it.

I then made plans for my trip to the west coast to once again see all of my Sisters, Brothers, Nieces, Nephews and Cousins after twenty-six years. I used my lifetime train pass and went to Vancouver first class there and back. I was met and picked up by my sister Irene; she took me home with her, stayed with her and her Husband for three weeks. They made sure that every moment was used up with pleasure and treated me like a Queen. There was sightseeing everyday and everywhere you could get to by automobile. Let me tell you it was truly wonderful and it is in my heart to stay for the rest of my life. Oh yes, they would not let me do any work of any kind while there, that was including not carrying shopping bags with groceries. What a wonderful couple they are, I love them so very much.

After that I went up to Prince George to be with another of my sisters, her name is Elizabeth, I stayed with her for one wonderful week. Also seen my niece Colleen and her family, what a beautiful family it is. Met and visited with my nephew Dennis and his family too, what a wonderful family they are. It was not only a great visit but a wonderful time to be remembered always, love them all dearly.

While away, my son Daniel took care of getting rid of the rest of the newspapers, fliers, magazines and a lot of other stuff. He knew I did not want any of it; he put it all in the recycling boxes and totes. The garbage men and recyclers must have thought we went bonkers again. When I returned home and found out how well he did for me, I went out and purchased a computer of his choice. This computer has dictating abilities as well as a copy machine to match. When we brought it home, Daniel put it all together himself in no time whatever and that made me even more proud of him.

Me, well I was frustrated with the computer so enrolled and attended a class in College, it was called "Basic Computers for Senior Adults." Truly had a great time and am not too bad at this thing now, oh I still make some goofs, who doesn't? Come January 2006 I will be taking another course "Basic Writing Skills." To bring you up to date, I passed the course with an A, had a real good time in class and a very good teacher. My next course starts February 21st. and is called "Writing Children's Books and Illustrations." This course will be truly tough for me as it has been a long time since I read books to my Sons. The final course in April to June is called "Introduction to Micro-Computers," it is already paid for and am ready to start anytime.

This Christmas 2005 I went to be with my son Fred and all his wonderful family. I took out the coin collection for the boys and gifts for everyone; went first class by train again. It was a very good trip and my eldest grandson Bradley was very upset when I left, he is so very precious to me. Coming home, the train was early and it waited for me, when I showed up they whisked me on really fast.

In June 2006 baring any ill health, I plan to take my grandson Bradley to a Blue Jay game. Then if all is well I will go to Stephenville to visit with cousins I have never met. Since finding them, I have kept in touch with them all. It is at the invitation of one couple that has given me the one thought, go; it will be a great trip I do know. Having not been back east since a small child, this will be a real challenge to me, I especially want to meet my namesake cousin Theresa.

If my health continues to hold up, I plan to go back to Vancouver to attend the Wedding of my niece Tine on August 5th. I am looking forward to that Wedding and also plan to stop in Calgary for a visit with my sister Marty in July, will take in the Stampede.. This will all depend on whether she wants me to come for a visit or not, only time will tell, I will get in touch with her first. Just to let you know, she does want me to come, so health being good, I will go.

Do you know what is simply wonderful to me? It is that I can once again make plans for my life, and return to learning. If God is willing maybe I will be able to take up my art again. All this and still wanting to do my Volunteer work too, not only do I give joy, I receive it in return. Am I expecting too much, I hope not. I am praying that my book will bring peace and joy as well as help to those who need it. This is the purpose for writing this book.

As you can see, I am doing and planning on doing as lot, in my estimation I believe that God has truly blessed me. I have all of my mental faculties and am able to take care of myself as well as help others, am also fully mobile. I would think before I did any running though, do not wish to push the heart too far. Now all I need to do is find a good publisher for this book and believe I already have. I have already sent in two payments so that it will be published in June, World Wide.

God has truly blessed me and may He do the same for you, all you have to do is believe. His Love for you will be with you, once you feel it, it is always there and so is the joy that goes with it. Your heart will be full at all times, when it is, you will talk to me as if I am there with you. The same as when you feel the joy of His Love, you will talk to Him. There is no greater Love than the "Lords." Joy Always!!!

ISBN 141209629-4

9 781412 096294